RETURN TO LIFE

A NEW LOOK AT THE PORTRAIT BUST

Selected and introduced by

PENELOPE CURTIS | PETER FUNNELL

NICOLA KALINSKY

With essays by

MALCOLM BAKER | JOHN GAGE

An exhibition produced by

HENRY MOORE INSTITUTE, LEEDS

NATIONAL PORTRAIT GALLERY, LONDON AND

SCOTTISH NATIONAL PORTRAIT GALLERY, EDINBURGH

THE PORTRAIT BUST is a much neglected form, despite its long historic prestige. We have forgotten how to read the bust, never mind look at it, and this is largely because it seems so formulaic. This exhibition invites us to look more closely at a formula which could, in fact, provide licence for a range of subtle and inventive variations. Specially commissioned photography takes us close to some of the key decisions made by the sculptors represented here, and focuses on the treatment of eyes, skin and musculature as well as on the choices made in the overall design.

An introduction by the three curators describes the exhibits in terms of their part in a sequential and pluralistic 'conversation' with the other works on show. Two new essays, by Malcolm Baker and John Gage, provide stimulating accounts of the historic settings – or 'installations' – of the sculpted bust in terms of establishing communal identity, and of specific relationships between sitter and sculptor, the head and its representation.

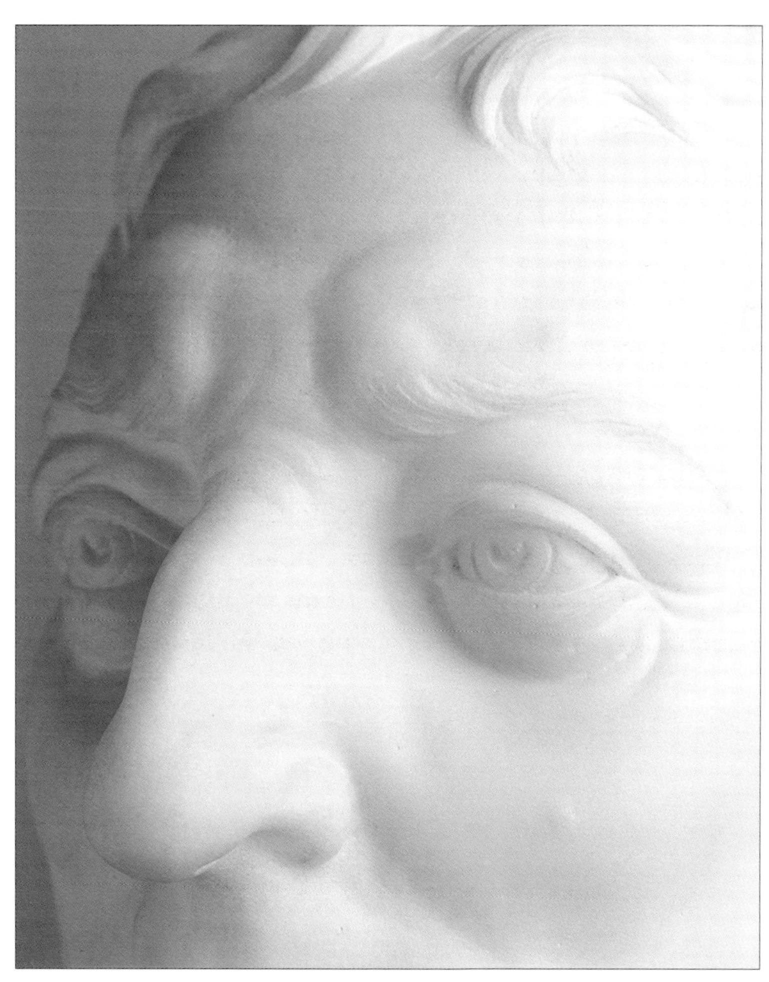

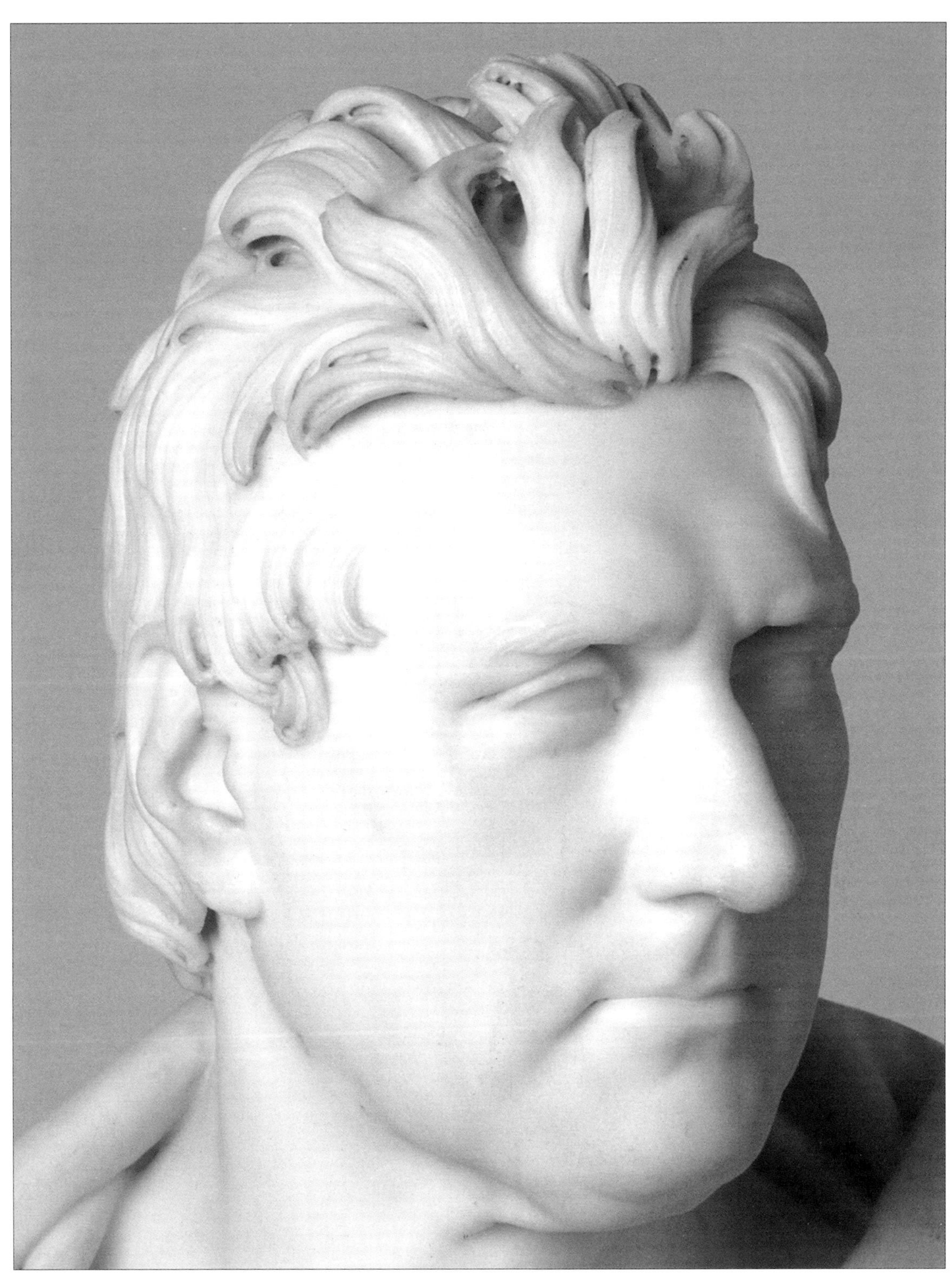

CONTENTS

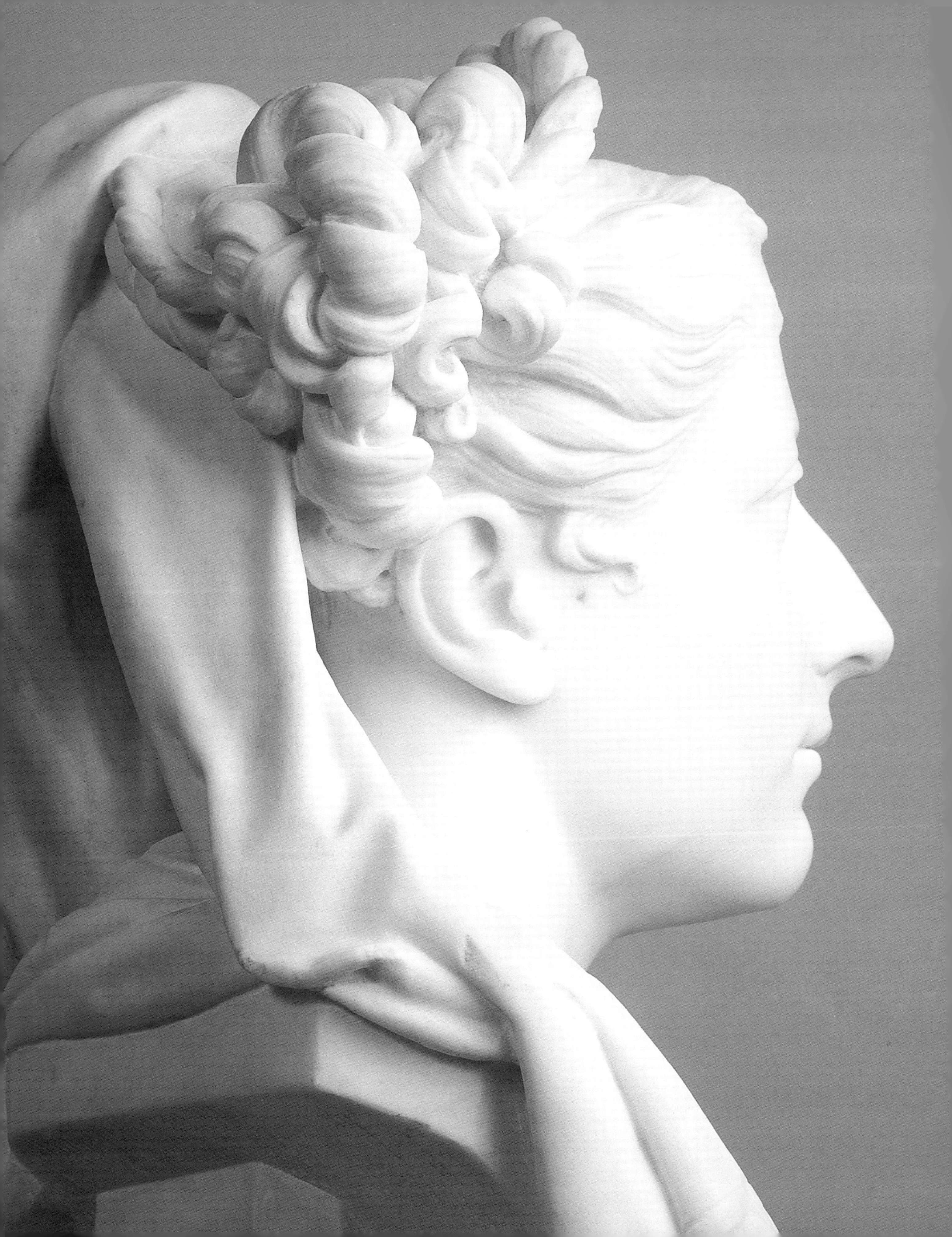

INTRODUCTION

BY THE CLOSE of the twentieth century, British visual art – contemporary and historical – had secured a new status; in particular, the opening of major displays and dedicated galleries has aroused considerable public and media interest. But this high visibility does not extend to all kinds of artistic production and one type which remains, literally and figuratively, in the background is the portrait bust – the sculpted representation of an individual's head. Neglected as a 'museum object', not often looked at as an art form and well outside the mainstream of contemporary creative expression in the last fifty years, the portrait bust, if considered at all, appears inscrutable or irrelevant. Yet, only a century ago its presence was ubiquitous; the portrait bust attracted some of the country's best artists and its demise would have been unthinkable.

This exhibition has its origins in the decision of three curators working from three different institutions to explore this phenomenon. Each curates a collection which contains portrait busts and in each institution the marginalisation of the portrait bust is apparent, to a greater or lesser extent. In both the National Portrait Gallery in London and the Scottish National Portrait Gallery in Edinburgh the institutions' remit of collecting depictions of historically significant individuals has led to large holdings of portrait busts. Whilst both display a number of these (although not in proportions which reflect the form's past popularity) and recent rehangs have attempted to reintegrate them, their presence in the portrait gallery remains problematic. If used to punctuate and dignify gallery spaces, portrait busts tend to lose their individuality and acquire, as decorative objects, an additional veil of invisibility. It seems much easier to view a portrait painting, either as a representation of an individual or as a work of art, than a sculpted portrait, which, ironically, at the time of making probably seemed to offer the most permanent personal memorial in a form with unimpeachable artistic credentials.

The situation in Leeds is not identical and thus enabled us to tackle the issue from a broader base. The Henry Moore Institute curates the sculpture holdings of Leeds Museums & Galleries, a more conventional fine art collection, where busts have normally been acquired because of their maker and their artistic importance rather than as representations of particular sitters. The Henry Moore Institute too, in its role as an advocate for the better understanding of sculptural practice and production, was the ideal partner to help the two nationals concentrate on an aspect of their collections which is rarely considered in its own right outside the parameters of the monograph.

Starting from no preconceived explanation for the portrait bust's decline into relative obscurity, we set ourselves the task of studying all the examples in all three collections – several hundred works. This process was stimulating beyond our expectations, the resistant form yielding to this concentrated and considerable exercise in looking. Our approach – three people with different interests and specialisms, yet naturally all representative in some way of the norms of modern curatorship – produced many insights and a shared sense of what we wanted to communicate. Looking led to considering and discussing, resulting in a far greater appreciation of the portrait bust, derived not from the usual curatorial process of one individual's absorption and reconsideration of given histories, but from an empirical and shared activity. The show aims to replicate this experience in condensed form, not so much as a presentation of our 'conclusions' but as an opportunity for visitors to engage in some of the visual and perceptual explorations which we found so stimulating. The face-to-face dialogue – between viewer and portrait bust, sculpted head and sculpted head, and visitors in conversation – is itself the process which revivifies the object and animates our understanding.

Our main aim in this exhibition is to concentrate on the works themselves but we also wished to open the exhibition by providing a basic historical platform for more free-ranging observations. This takes the form of four symbolic examples from across the period which seemed to us to embody the primary functions and suggest the typical locations of the portrait bust at particular points in time.

The first of these, chosen to evoke a normative place and use, is John Cheere's plaster of *Cicero*, a 'library bust'. Libraries were among the most important setting for busts in the eighteenth century both in private houses and educational institutions. Of the latter, Trinity College, Cambridge and Trinity College, Dublin are notable examples and, as was the convention, display busts of both ancient and modern figures. Those considered appropriate to signify the different forms of learning represented in the library itself – whether Homer or Seneca from the ancient world or Milton and Newton from the more recent past – came to form a canon of worthies repeated from library to library. As this suggests, these were often produced as 'multiples', with Cheere himself emerging by the middle of the eighteenth century as the foremost purveyor. His bust of the Roman statesman, orator and writer Cicero, from Temple Newsam House, Leeds, was probably part of a set of library

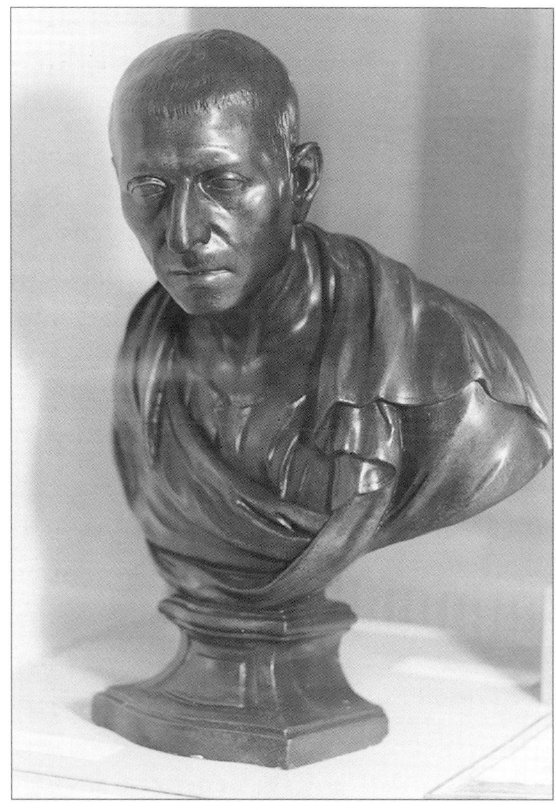

Cicero

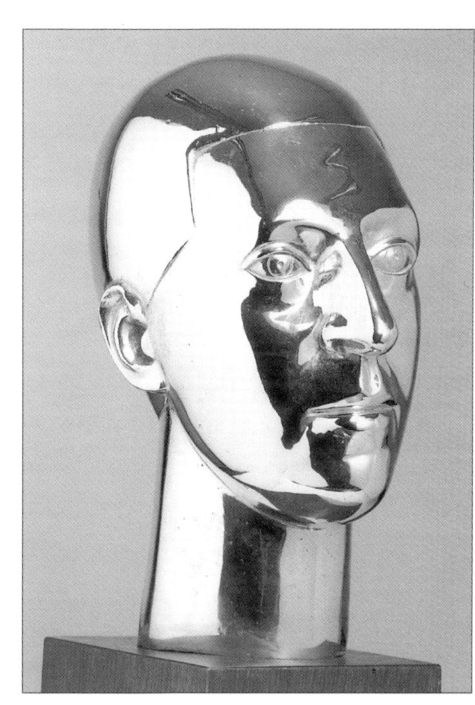

Sir Osbert Sitwell

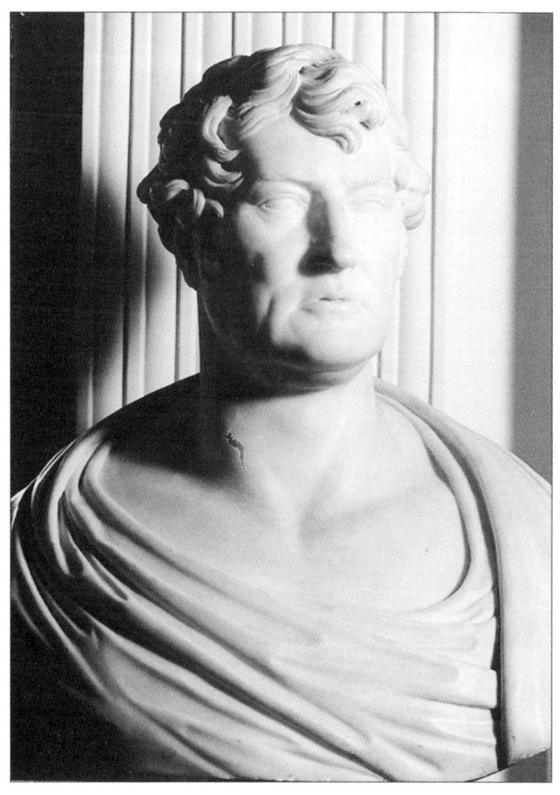

George Banks

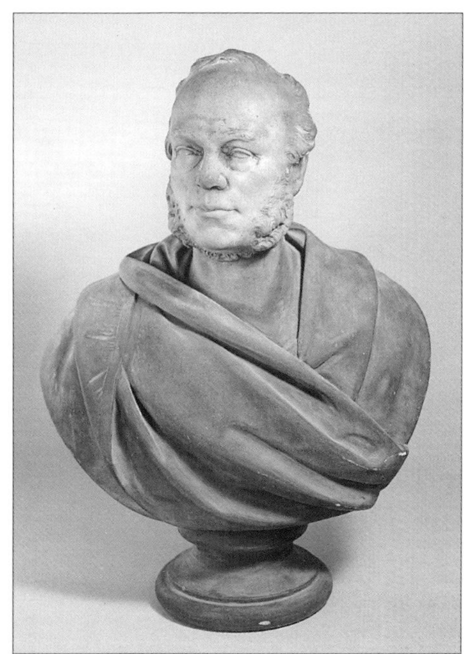

Unknown Man

busts and is known in at least four other similar versions. Drawing upon a repertoire of conventional images of Cicero, it recreates the classical form which was to dominate the portrait bust in Britain – figures from the past and present – for the next century and a half.

Exemplifying the continued adherence to the classical formula in the nineteenth century is the bust of *George Banks* by Joseph Gott. Here, partially bare-chested with toga-like draperies, is a northern industrialist and civic leader. It is, perhaps, this apparent dissonance between the classical model and its use to portray an individual of fairly ordinary origins that so distances such busts from us today. Nonetheless the bust of Banks seemed to us to demonstrate nineteenth-century trends precisely because the form was considered an appropriate way to represent such middle-class figures. Moreover Banks himself, with his wide range of public activities, epitomises the civic and institutional developments which took place in Britain's regions and which in turn helped to foster the demand for the portrait bust. A mayor of Leeds, a member of the Leeds Volunteers, a founder member of the Leeds Philosophical and Literary Society and a member of the Northern Society for the Encouragement of the Fine Arts, Banks' interests reflect an age when involvement in such associations became an important aspect of middle-class male behaviour and identity. And although apparently a private commission by Banks himself, Gott's assertively masculine portrait very much presents an image of the public man.

By contrast, Frank Dobson's remarkable *Osbert Sitwell* introduces a very different public sphere which the bust can be said to have occupied in the twentieth century: the art exhibition or gallery. Within just a year or so of its completion, the original version of this bust entered the Tate Gallery collection and was subsequently seen at exhibitions such as the Venice Biennale of 1928. Throughout almost its entire history, the contexts in which

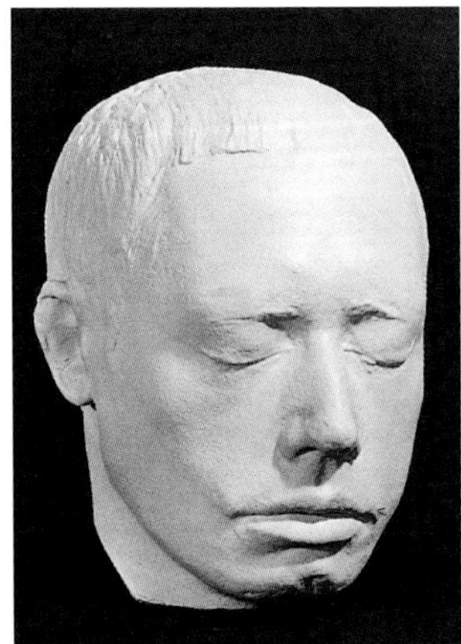

Life Mask

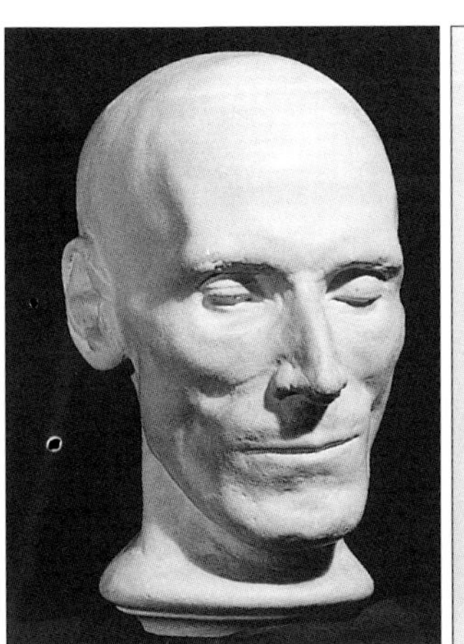

George Combe

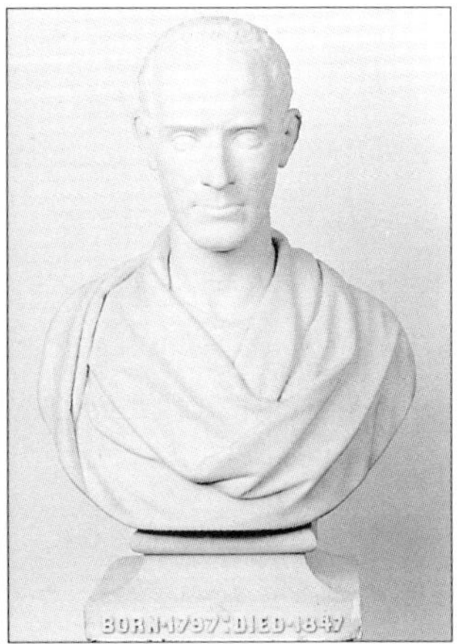

Death Mask

Dr Andrew Combe

this bust has been seen have reinforced its aura as a work of art rather than its status as a piece of portraiture. With its pared down, almost streamlined features and shiny surface, *Sitwell* shows how, in the early part of the twentieth century, the portrait bust could be a vehicle for emphatically artistic invention. Indeed, in the ten or twenty years before World War Two, the bust enjoyed something of a renaissance as its basic form was reinvented by the European avant-garde. Only after this time have modernist sculptors departed so conspicuously from the tradition of the portrait bust.

This part of the introductory section of the exhibition concludes with a bust presented in the condition we found it in the store room of the Leeds City Art Gallery, an example – which we could have chosen from any of our collections – which vividly demonstrates the degree to which this prestigious art form has fallen out of favour. Doubtless of some worthy individual similar to Banks, the bust has now lost its identity. Poorly regarded as a work of art, it no longer even functions as a likeness of a known individual.

As a coda to this contextual background, we have included busts of two nineteenth-century sitters – the brothers *George Combe* and *Dr Andrew Combe* – alongside their life and death masks. This section of the exhibition is intended to question how art differs from more 'literal' representations by making a simple contrast between portrait busts and casts taken directly from their subjects either in life or death. George and Andrew Combe were, respectively, an Edinburgh lawyer and physician and both were leading advocates of phrenology – the belief current in the middle years of the nineteenth century that the shape of the skull, itself reflective of the physical characteristics of the brain within, revealed an individual's personality.

———

The main part of the exhibition is divided into two: *The General Design* and *The Face and its Features*. We see these sections as dialogues; each bust leads onto the next one, but also makes reference to others in the 'conversation'. The selection, necessarily concentrated, nevertheless represents both the recurrent and the salient features which emerged from looking across the collections more widely. The busts which made it to the final selection are those to which we kept coming back, their design or their features sufficiently impressed upon our memories to act not so much as anomalies, but as benchmarks for the discussion of the form.

The General Design looks at the overall shape of the bust, how the head fits onto the shoulders, and how both are supported. The following descriptions, charting the works in each section, are intended not to exhaust the readings of each bust, but to suggest and summarise the key role which each piece plays within the primary 'conversation'.

Joseph Nollekens' *Charles James Fox* is a good example of the male torso becoming the sculptural support, in this strange marriage of body and base. Fox's naked 'breastplate' is mounted onto a small socle, carrying the conceit one step further.

By contrast, in George MacCallum's *David Bryce*, the naked breast is brought solidly into contact with the plinth, as if body had really been turned into marble. The breasts provide a curved section, almost book-like in its profile.

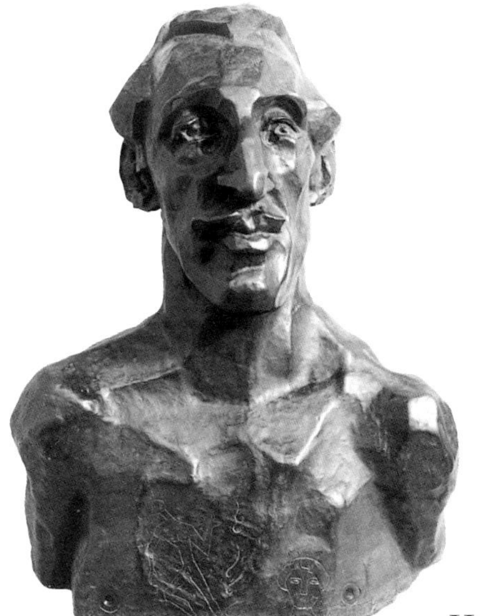

Henri Gaudier-Brzeska's bust of *Horace Brodzky*, seen as a fine example of modernist portraiture, picks up on this notion of allowing the upper body to become the sculpture's base, prioritising material over subject, the inanimate over the animate. The bust is also incised, as if it were just matter, and in this again refers back to a more ancient tradition.

The solid frontality of these busts is extended and developed in Jacob Epstein's *George Black*, but now the body is clothed and folded arms provide an unusually substantial base for the form.

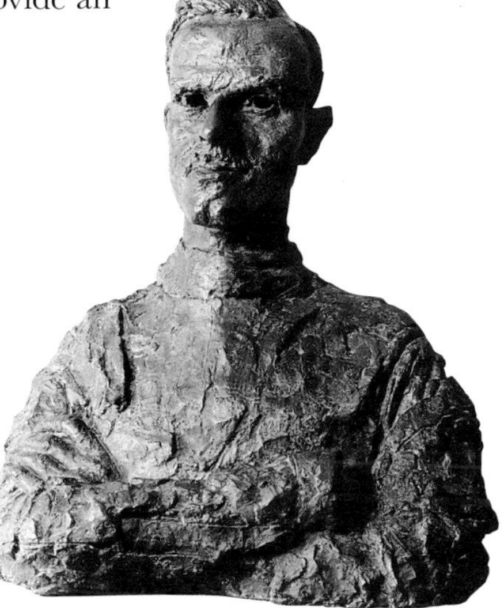

In *Margaret Rawlings*, Frank Dobson also depicts the arms, and now, in keeping with a female subject, uses them to alleviate a possibly assertive frontality and to pull the viewer's eye around the form, moving round to meet the sitter's own gaze.

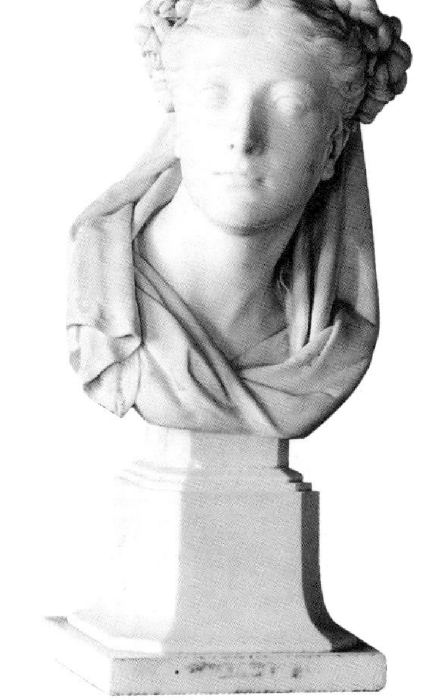

A similarly non-frontal lyricism is captured by Samuel Joseph in his bust of *Miss Ramsay ?*, which also uses accessories, in this case an inventive draped hair-style and inversely rhyming socle, to add outward movement to his portrait.

Albert Toft's *Robert Bontine Cunninghame Graham* effects a dynamic contrapposto, in which the head is turned almost fully to one side, and the gaze directed away from the viewer.

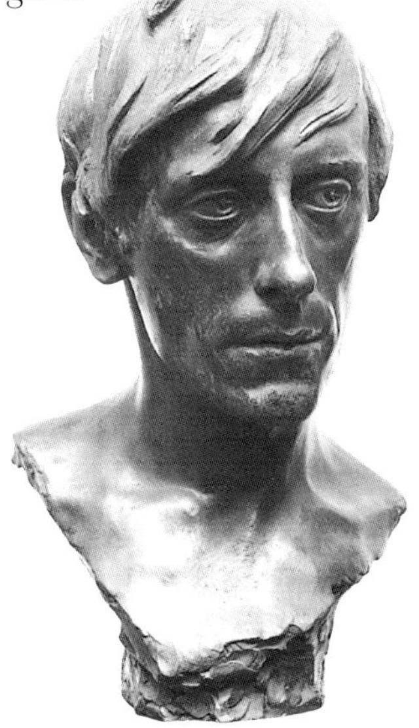

Francis Derwent Wood's *Ambrose McEvoy* shows a much less dynamic version of the 'torn' bronze neckline. *McEvoy* has an air of modesty, with its very slight turn, reduced base and slightly vacant gaze.

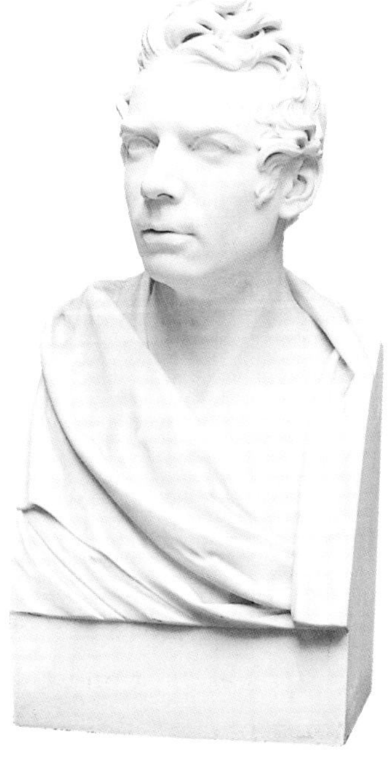

Joseph's *Sir David Wilkie* restores the upper torso to the bust, now clad in drapery as a transitional zone between head and socle. Realism – and movement – are sharply contained within the clearly demarcated base.

John Rhind's *Professor Sir John Leslie* brings us back to a fully frontal representation, in which a 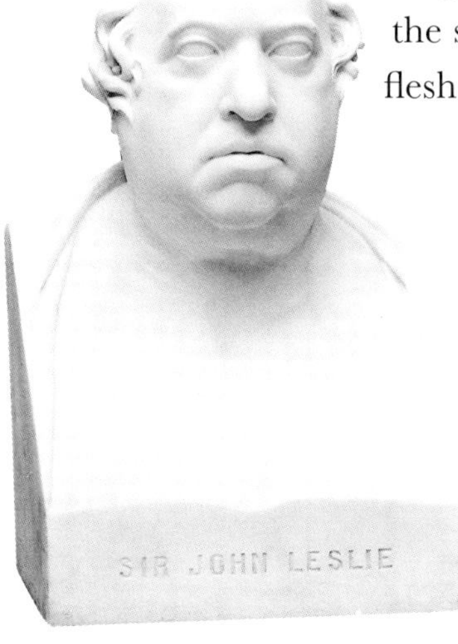 still realistic rendering of neck and upper torso are offset by merely vestigial drapery and the massiveness of the naked base on which the subject's name is now inscribed, making clear the passing of flesh into marble.

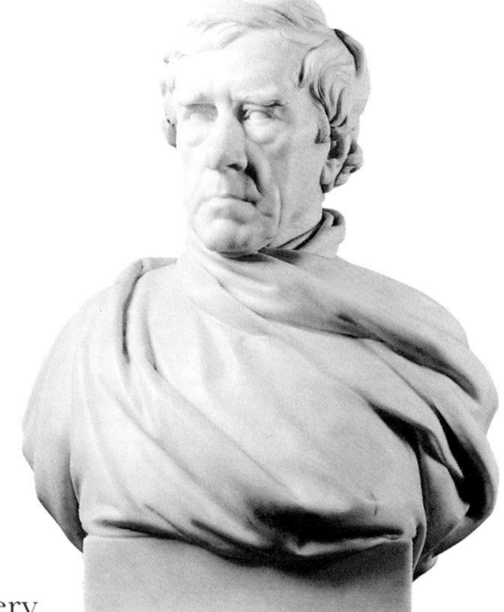

John Adams Acton's *Henry Peter Brougham*, uses drapery to unusual effect, completely swathing the torso, and suggesting a dynamism which is echoed in the face. The movement of the cloth is restrained by the severe modesty of the base itself.

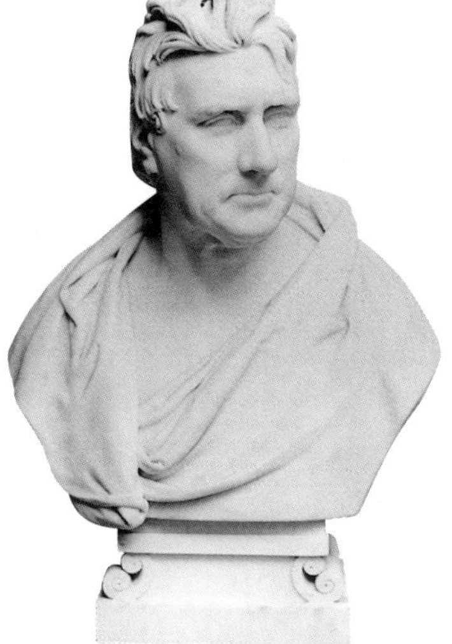

This contained dynamism is picked up by Sir Francis Leggatt Chantrey's *John Rennie*, a near 'typical' bust, in which the body emerges from an unremarkable amount of drapery, clearly separated from sculptural support. The slight movement of the head off-centre, and the downward cast of a firmly directed gaze, represented a model that was often repeated, if rarely so successfully.

Face and Features narrows the focus, looking at surface, texture and the separate elements that make up a human head. Joseph Wilton's *William Pitt,* is a standard classical bust, frontal and fairly static, but made vigorous through the intensely detailed musculature of the face, with a busy surface seeming to represent both the life of the mind and its outward manifestation.

Henry Weekes' *Hugh Richard Fahie Hoare* represents a young boy with smooth unformed features. Combined with the knowledge of his premature death, we read this as an 'ideal' portrait representative of unrealised potential.

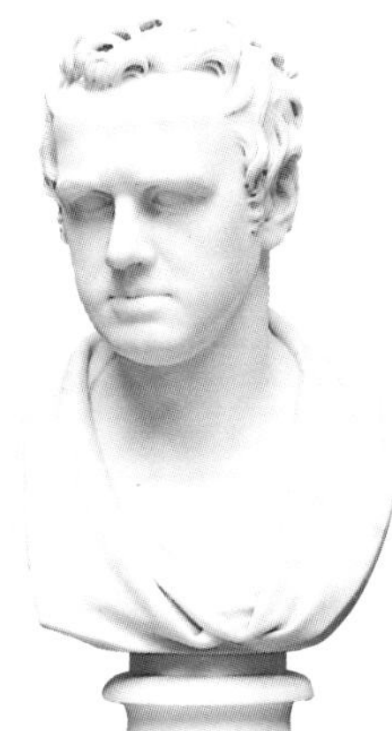

Chantrey's *Francis Horner* shows a more or less idealised face, hovering between youth and maturity, at once firm and yet undecided.

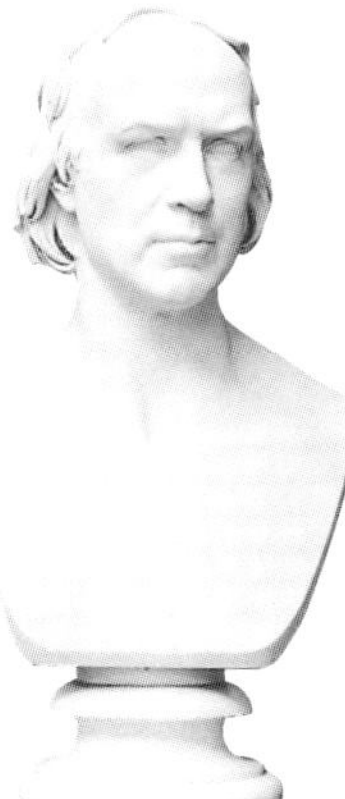

Weekes' *Allan Cunningham* represents, with seemingly judicious realism, a man at the prime of life, dignified but modest.

Joseph's *Henry MacKenzie* might be contrasted to the boyish *Hoare*, the youthful *Horner*, and the mature *Cunningham*. This face is marked by time in obvious contrast to that of *Hoare*. Although it could never be termed idealistic, it might be seen to represent the typology of 'old age', much as *Hoare* represents a standardised 'youth'.

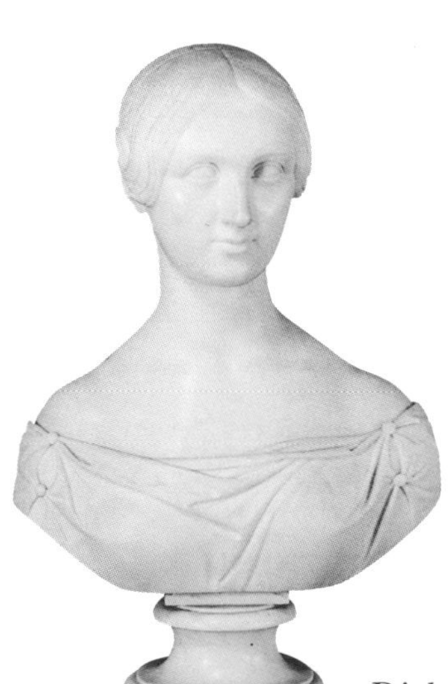

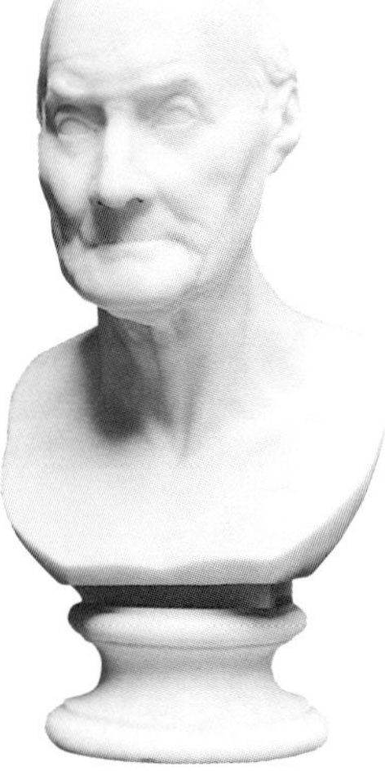

Richard James Wyatt's *Bust of a Woman* epitomises the crossover between commissioned portraiture and idealised representation. To what extent we should read the smooth, apparently undistinctive features as typical, rather than specific, is difficult to assess.

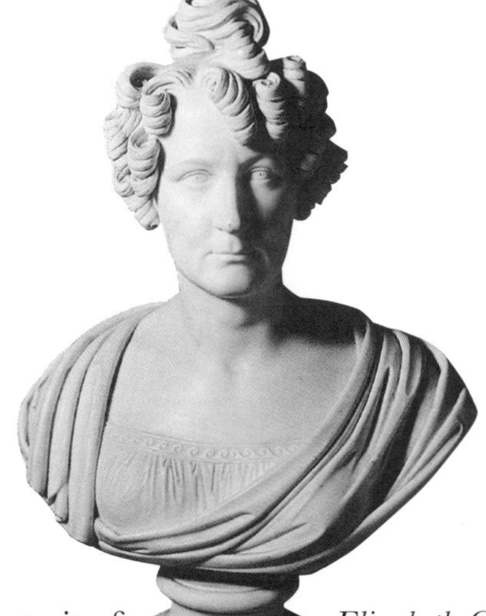

In contrast, Joseph Gott's portrait of *Elizabeth Goodman Banks* is strikingly specific, active, and engaged. This is not achieved so much through the straightforwardly realistic treatment as by the directness of a gaze set free by a comfortably balanced overall pose.

Jacob Epstein's *Lady Gregory* is equally specific, but here the gaze seems to turn in on itself, giving the effect of both an inner life and of the hollowness behind the mask.

Masks bear an interesting and ever-present relationship to portraiture, to which the section with the Combe brothers makes allusion. Kathleen Scott's *John Galsworthy* suggests itself as a direct cast from life, but also has something deathly in its interiorised, almost other-worldly quality.

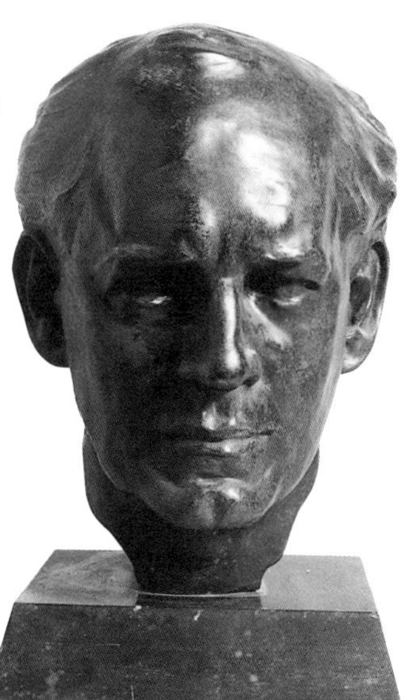

David Evans' *John Galsworthy* is very different, piercing us with the intensity of its look rather in the manner of ancient Roman portraiture. The frontal aspect and crisp delineation of the features suggest something of the anatomical study, somehow avoiding the inner life of the sitter.

Patric Park's *James Jardine* is mask-like in another sense. Veiled as if its features were literally lying behind their marble coating, its waxy aspect has a disturbing quality.

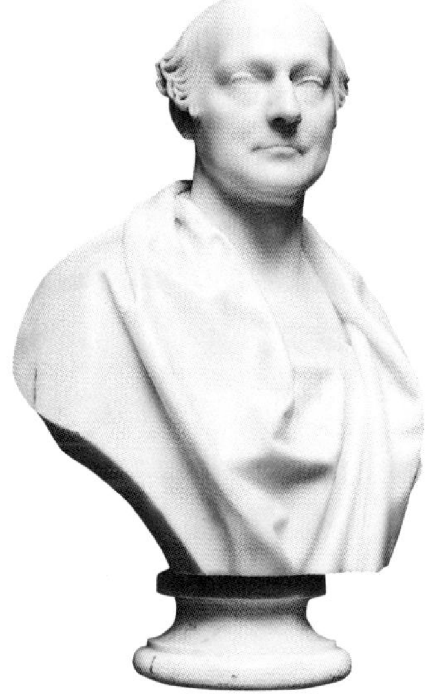

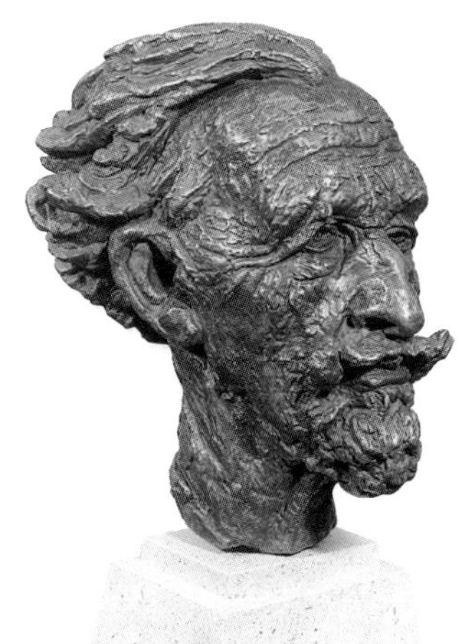

The surface of Epstein's *Cunninghame Graham* is similarly thick, but the features emerge with great clarity, as if they were cut through the heavily worked skin which lies, like a kind of pelt, over the skull.

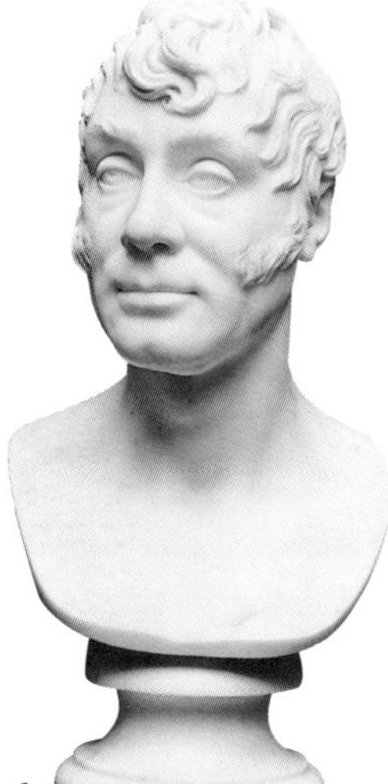

Nollekens' *James Maitland,* returns us to a face which seems to be that of a man of both thought and action. The eyes are semi-veiled, the mouth, poised between silence and speech, the whole, a disciplined combination which seems to represent the marriage of supporting material and surface treatment, of the inner and outer man.

Penelope Curtis | Peter Funnell | Nicola Kalinsky

'A SORT OF CORPORATE COMPANY'

APPROACHING THE
PORTRAIT BUST IN ITS SETTING

How can we approach the portrait bust? The question is in part a conceptual one, challenging us to resolve the dilemma posed by a highly conventionalised type of sculpture that is now at once very familiar and yet distant. Busts are often present in the spaces around us, whether as part of the aspirational décor of rooms illustrated in *The World of Interiors*, or populating the public spaces – inside and outside – of most urban centres. Yet, for viewers today, portrait busts have become part of these settings rather than images to be considered and engaged with in their own right. What were conceived of as speaking likenesses have become invisible faces. One way of 'approaching the portrait bust' is to address this tension. But 'approaching' also suggests the idea of 'getting nearer' – coming into a closer physical and spatial relationship with the subject. To make sense of the bust and reclaim it as a mode of representation that has distinctive visual interest and authority therefore requires us to engage not simply with busts alone, but with busts and their settings. This might seem rather abstract, even paradoxical, but we can make it feel less so by taking a walk and approaching some portrait busts in two very different but geographically close settings, on opposite sides of Lincoln's Inn Fields in central London.

One line of approach would be to go half way along the south side of Lincoln's Inn Fields and enter the Royal College of Surgeons.[1] On coming into the entrance hall, we find ourselves in the presence of a group of busts, arranged regularly on plinths around this communal social space. Relatively recent changes have relocated some images in other rooms and, as a view taken in 1912 shows (FIG.1), the impression of a hall populated by marble would have been still more pronounced during the nineteenth and early twentieth centuries. Ahead of us is the seated figure of John Hunter whose anatomical investigations in part led to the recognition of surgery as a profession and the establishment of the College under Royal charter in 1800. But loosely associated with this single dominant statue are the many busts, arranged to fit in with the architecture which they both articulate and animate. These, however, we do not notice individually; instead, they make their presence felt in an additive and cumulative way. Above all, they seem to 'belong'. Despite the apparent qualities of sculptural portraits as a form of representation that addresses a public audience, these works are not in a public place. Their association and setting together here signals a kinship not only between the sitters represented but also between them and most of those who viewed them – other Fellows of the College. Precisely because in their materials and conventions portrait busts can so easily be regarded as the same, they together reinforce the impression of belonging. As we look at them – with our visitor passes labelling us more prominently than them – we register them collectively, as part of the building that speaks of institutional authority.

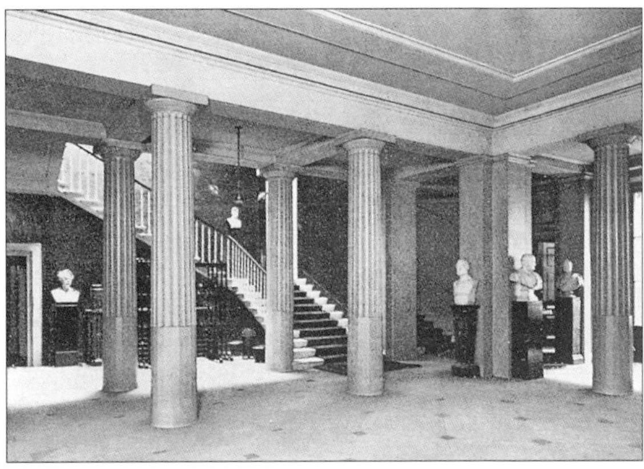

Fig.1 **Royal College of Surgeons Hall and Staircase**
1912
© V & A Picture Library, London

A very different line of approach opens up if we walk along the north side of Lincoln's Inn Fields and enter Sir John Soane's Museum.[2] In the hallway we can choose between a number of possible ways to take through the architect's house but, whichever route we take, it will lead to the Dome – the open space that stretches from the basement to conical skylight and houses the densely arranged collection of antique and Egyptian sculpture and architectural fragments, both casts and originals. Amid this packed display, our eye is caught first by the cast of the *Apollo Belvedere*, placed at one end, but then by the marble bust of Soane himself, set opposite *Apollo* on the balustrade (FIG.2). Despite the abundance of material that surrounds it, Soane's bust is not simply one more piece but, on the contrary, is perceived to be at the heart of the house, prompting us to see it as an authoritative directing presence. Having glimpsed the bust when we entered the Dome, we then engage with it as a single dominant image and understand the rest of the house – the collections and the architectural achievement it celebrates – as the outcome of the imagination it represents. The bust is placed so that it is not abutted or impinged upon by other objects but rather set quite high within its own free space. Such a setting – framed yet isolated – encourages us to think that we are coming face to face with Soane as an individual. By the time the bust was installed in this position, the house was already open to the public and, like most busts, this marble was from the start conceived of as a public image. As Byron remarked, drawing a contrast between sculptural and painted portraits, 'a bust ... smacks something of a hankering for public fame rather than private remembrance.'[3] Yet our viewing of the bust of Soane involves a mode of engagement that is essentially private.

Although these portrait busts – whether those in the Royal College of Surgeons or that of Soane – were not made as site-specific works, they nonetheless were (and are) viewed and responded to within their different settings. If one tension apparent in our approach to the portrait bust involves its simultaneous existence as a particular and distinct

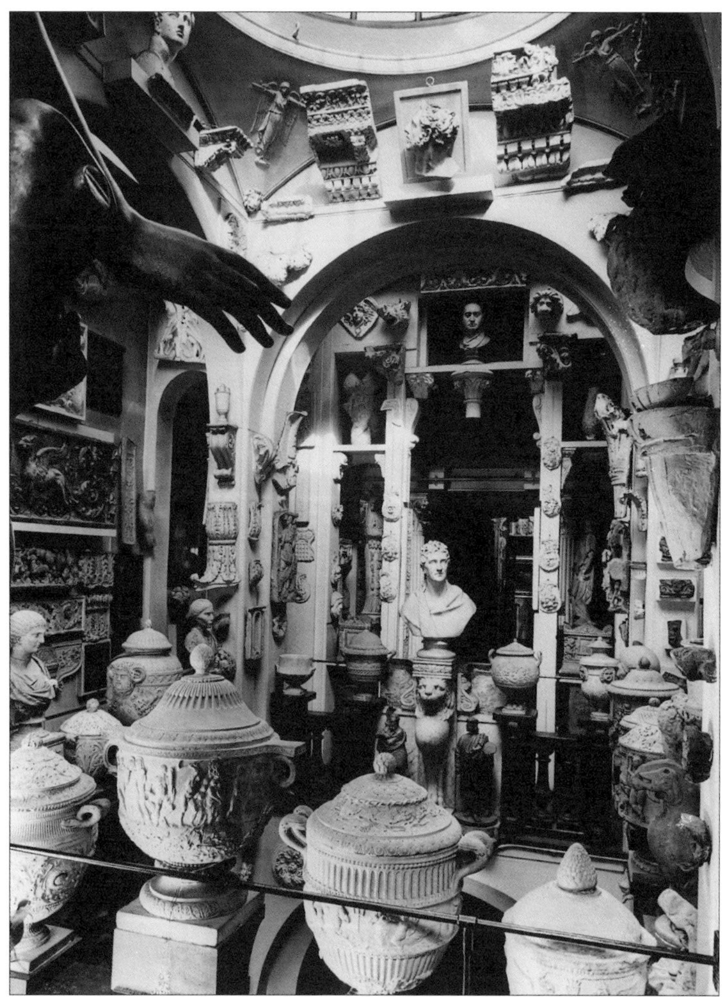

Fig. 2 Sir Francis Leggatt Chantrey (1781–1841)
Sir John Soane, in the Dome, Sir John Soane's Museum
1830 Marble
By courtesy of the Trustees of the Sir John Soane's Museum, London

image and its almost seamless incorporation within an architectural setting, be it institutional (as at the Royal College) or highly personal (as in Soane's house), another tension consists of the play between the individual likeness, on the one hand, and group identity through a shared convention, on the other. Approaching the portrait bust means coming to terms with this latter tension as much as with the former. Entering a space where many busts are displayed challenges us to register them as part of a larger communal whole – members, as it were, of a club – while coming face to face with them as individual images.

Joining the Club

The most familiar club is, of course, the family and one important setting for portrait busts was as part of a sequence of family portraits in the hall or gallery of a country house. For eighteenth-century patrons, the use of busts of ancestors in this way was given antique authority by Roman practice. As Lord Bolingbroke put it:

> The citizens of Rome placed the images of their ancestors in the vestibules of their houses, so that, whenever they went in or out, these venerable busts met their eyes, and recalled the glorious actions of the dead to fire the living, to excite them to imitate, and even to emulate, their great forefathers. Their success answered the design. The virtue of one generation was transfused, by the magic of example, into several; and a spirit of heroism was maintained through many ages of that commonwealth.[4]

Recalling this and other Roman precedents, the placing of busts in a house from which the family estate was controlled served to make visible the continuity of lineage and property ownership. Arranged in this apparently natural, or at least familiar, way, such sequences of conventional images made clear to the viewer – whether family, guest, or tenant – the authority that was carried from generation to generation. But alongside these strictly ancestral portraits were set images of friends, their proximity registering their closeness to that family.

Among the Pembroke family portraits described in the various eighteenth-century guides to Wilton House were not only busts of the 9th Earl of Pembroke and his wife but also marbles of his fellow antiquarians and friends, Sir Andrew Fountaine and Martin Folkes, other versions of which were evidently given by the Earl to each of them as tokens of friendship. With their interest in Roman coins, Fountaine and Folkes, like Pembroke, were probably very alive to how they were being represented as sculptural images as well as to how their portrait busts were to be used. So too, no doubt, was another antiquarian whose bust was incorporated within an English aristocrat's family images. As a young man, the Florentine physician Dr Antonio Cocchi had come to England with Theophilus Hastings, 9th Earl of Huntingdon, and some thirty years later acted as a guide to the 10th Earl around the Florentine collections. The 10th Earl commissioned a bust of Cocchi and himself and, in the late eighteenth century, these were to be found in Donington Hall, Leicestershire, along with marbles of Pythagoras and other ancients.[5] Here, then, the juxaposition of busts of family and friends was merged with another established type of grouping, made up of authors and 'worthies'.

While family and friends might form one important context for busts, many other groupings were becoming possible from the early eighteenth century onwards. Belonging could mean, for instance, being a political ally, as at Stowe in the 1740s, where Lord

Cobham had himself represented amid his supporters.[6] In the Temple of Friendship, erected in the gardens to complement other structures with prominent sculptural elements such as the Temple of British Worthies and the Temple of Ancient Virtue, Cobham (FIG.3) and his fellow Whig 'patriots' were shown wearing Roman armour and short hair so signifying their adherence to the political virtues of ancient Rome. Incorporation into a family sequence or some other extended group could, naturally, have a bearing on the convention adopted by the sitter or sculptor, especially if the intended company or setting was known. But as well as sharing this same convention, the busts at Stowe were perceived as

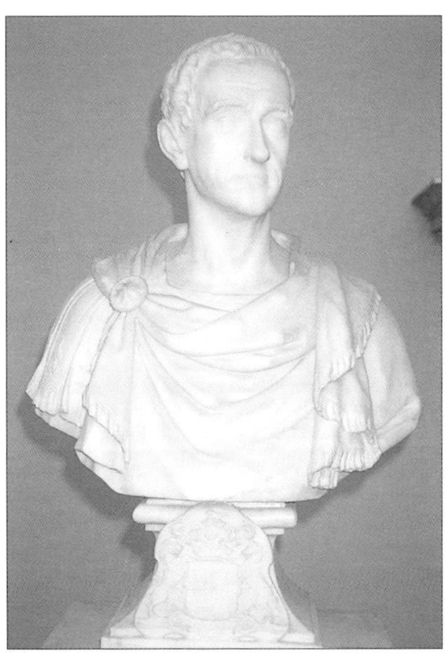

Fig.3 Peter Scheemakers
(1691–1781)
Viscount Cobham
c.1733 Marble
Victoria & Albert Museum,
London

belonging together through their placing on plinths set at regular intervals around the interior, their presence still indicated today by gaps in the plasterwork. In their original setting, before the Temple became a ruin, these busts would have been given a context within a national history through being placed below a ceiling decorated with scenes from the periods of Edward III and Elizabeth I in which 'British' political liberty and patriotic virtues were seen to match those of the Roman republic.

Around sixty years later another Whig patron, Francis, 5th Duke of Bedford, placed a bust of himself amid political figures such as Charles James Fox, in the Temple of Liberty at Woburn, the sitters all similarly shown in classical dress.[7] While such assemblages of busts in settings specifically designed primarily for their display may have been exceptional, the association of a patron's sculptural image with busts of friends or political allies was one of the most familiar uses of sculpture in the late eighteenth and early nineteenth centuries. No other individual however, was in a position to do as the Duke of Wellington did when he introduced sculpture into the staircase at Apsley House. Having acquired the colossal nude figure of Napoleon, executed by Canova for the emperor before his defeat by Wellington at Waterloo, the Duke placed this at the foot of the grand spiral staircase. Then he set on brackets around the walls busts by Christian Daniel Rauch of those foreign rulers and generals whose forces, in concert with British troops, led to Napoleon's defeat.[8] Even the Duke of Marlborough, whose bombastic militarism was given prominent expression through sculpture at Blenheim Palace in the early eighteenth century, had not grouped portrait busts so as to form quite such a triumphant celebration of victory on the battlefield.

In all these cases the busts were chosen by a particular patron to be placed so as to define his own achievements, commitments and aspirations; an act of self-representation complementing those sequences of ancestral portraits in which a sitter takes his or her place within a narrative of family history, one component part in a sequential lineage. But, from the early eighteenth century onwards, busts could also be assembled and arranged as exemplars of virtue – in the widest possible sense – from the past. One form this could take is found in the Temple of British Worthies at Stowe and another in the more widely adopted series of author images deployed in eighteenth-century libraries, where ancients complemented moderns. Pantheons of 'worthies' appear with increasing frequency on the exterior of public buildings from the early nineteenth century onwards but by the mid nineteenth century another type of group was becoming common. Busts commemorating local figures – both historical and contemporary –were placed in the newly erected municipal buildings of many expanding provincial towns and cities. Set prominently in architecture that spoke of provincial wealth and pride, these groups of portrait busts were one of the most telling signs of civic and local identity. As such, they were one of the nineteenth century's preferred categories of visual representation. Indeed, nothing seems so eminently Victorian as a line of marble busts in a town hall.

The busts that survive in the Shire Hall in Taunton may stand as an example of this, albeit an unusually well-documented and somewhat idiosyncratic case. Two years after the completion of the Early Tudor style building in 1858 by Gilbert Scott's former partner, W. B. Moffatt, Robert Arthur Kinglake, a local JP, succeeded in his efforts to have erected there Baily's 'colossal bust in statuary marble of the great Admiral Blake, supported on a terminal pedestal of Sicilian marble, enriched at the summit with trophies indicative of his career as a military and naval commander.'[9] Although this was initially seen as a temporary location for what Lord Macaulay (whose support Kinglake had sought) called 'the best Memorial of the Defender of Taunton', it was joined shortly afterwards by busts of the philosopher, John Locke, born at Wrington in Somerset; Thomas Ken, the seventeenth-century non-juror Bishop of Bath and Wells; Henry Byam, Chaplain to both Charles I and II; and the Parliamentarian, John Pym. Several of these busts were by London sculptors such as Baily or E. G. Papworth but others were by productive local firms of mason-sculptors, such as Tyleys of Bristol.

Despite the objection from a fellow magistrate, that he was setting up 'graven images of second-rate nobodies', Kinglake's energetic efforts to create a 'Valhalla of Somerset Worthies' continued unabated and over the next ten years an already somewhat miscellaneous assembly was enlarged to include busts of the orientalist and linguist, Edwin Norris; Queen Victoria's physician, Wilson Fox; John Hanning Speke, the explorer of the Nile; the general, John Jacob; the novelist, Henry Fielding, and, rather surprisingly, the sculptor of Norris' bust, Charles Summers, who had worked in Australia and Rome but was a native of Weston-super-Mare. In assembling what the poet Austin Dobson called 'that provincial Prytaneum', Kinglake was consciously following Bolingbroke's recommendation and prefaced his pamphlet, *Somerset Worthies*, with the passage quoted above. Kinglake published an expanded version of his essay – 'the story of the Somerset Valhalla, its rise and progress' – in 1891 and thirty years after the start of his project was claiming that although the 'hall itself is now full ... the vestibule is capable of holding many more busts, and even a full-length statue of King Alfred'. While this last was not executed, the sixteen busts collectively animate the interior of the Shire Hall, complementing its historicising style through this somewhat bizarre series of figures from the County's past. Even if we take account of Kinglake's admission that he may have seemed 'over zealous in the attainment of my object', the presence of this assemblage was certainly registered by contemporaries to the extent that the half-page entry on Taunton in Baedecker's 1906 guide to Great Britain singles the series out for attention.[10] What is striking is how a grouping of busts that formed such a prominent feature of an interior to observers in 1906 could, within fifty years, become completely overlooked.

The fact that, although subsequently neglected, the Shire Hall busts have remained *in situ* might suggest that, once set up, busts continue to commemorate their sitters in perpetuity, as their patrons and sculptors had planned and that this process has a natural inevitability. Often, however, this was not the case at all. Even at the start, the placing of a portrait bust and the company it was to keep could be a contentious issue. Setting up a bust and so making a claim for a sitter's virtues and achievements could itself prompt dissent and where it was to be placed could be the cause of still more protest. An awareness of these sorts of dispute was assumed by the cartoonist James Sayer when he showed Nollekens' bust of the politician Charles James Fox being placed by Catherine II of Russia in a niche between statues of Cicero and Demosthenes in her gallery (FIG.4). Here, the two ancient exemplars of civic virtue and probity take exception to being joined by the (to some eyes) far more dubious Fox. Busts did not, of course, always remain in the same place and new conjunctions could be made. In some cases a new setting could reinforce an already implicit association. The craggy image of Daniel Finch, 2nd Earl of Nottingham – a sculptural portrait that brings to mind Henry James' phrase, 'the bristling surface of his actuality'[11] – seems to have made reference to Roman busts then believed to represent Julius

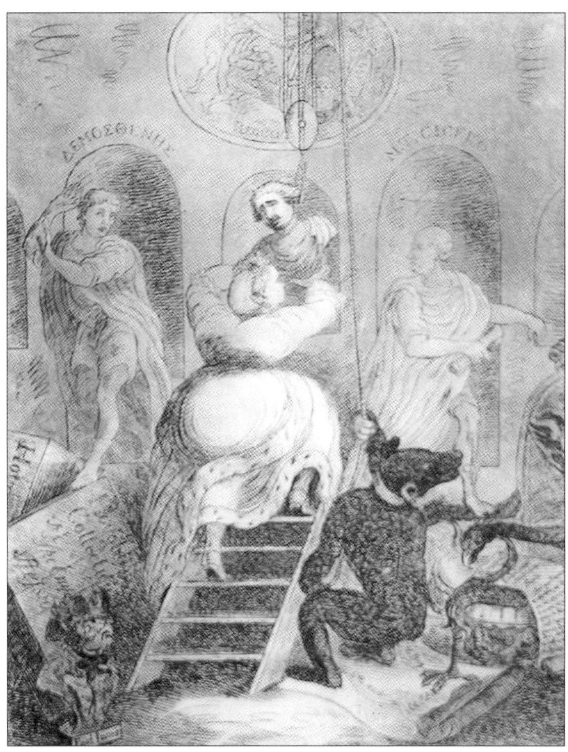

Fig.4 James Sayer (1748–1828)
The Patriot Exalted
1792, etching and aquatint
Victoria & Albert Museum, London

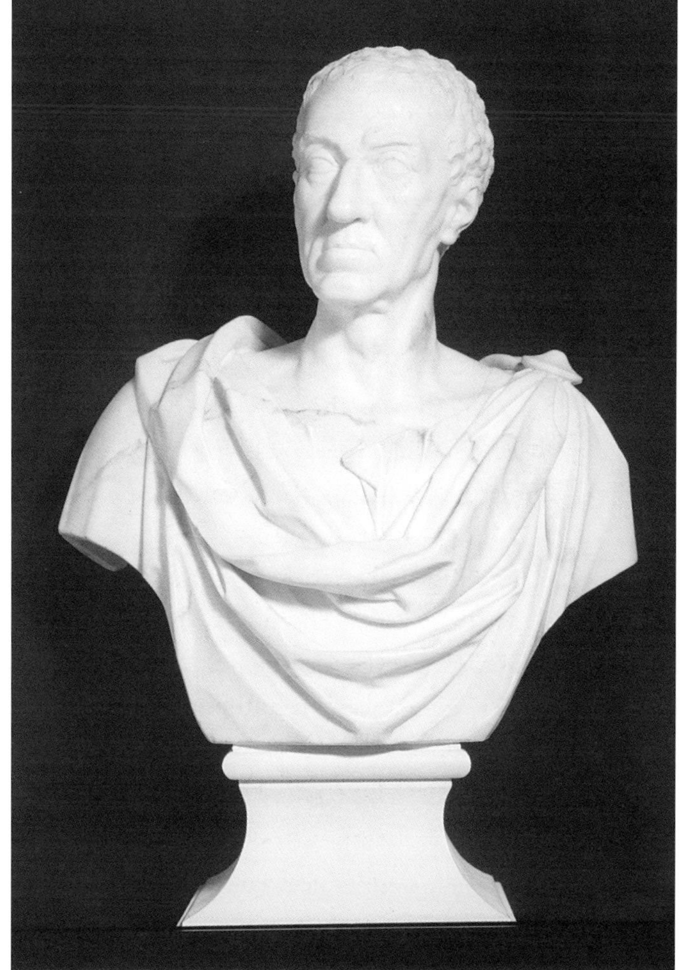

Fig.5 John Michael Rysbrack (1684–1770)
Daniel Finch, 2nd Earl of Nottingham
1723 Marble
Victoria & Albert Museum, London

Caesar (FIG.5). While the marble was in his second son's house in London, the classicising convention being explored here did not necessarily connect with the setting, but, when moved to the foot of the stairs in the family house at Burley-on-the-Hill in Rutland, it could be read in terms of a relationship with scenes from the life of Caesar that the viewer would have encountered on the walls of the saloon on the floor above.[12]

Moving busts around could create different configurations of meaning and different narratives. Nowhere is this more vividly illustrated than by the different settings used for the bust of Soane which now seems so much at home in the Dome of his Museum. Given by Chantrey to the sitter 'as a mark of esteem', the marble was highly regarded by the sculptor – 'as a work of art I have never produced a better' – and was shown by him at the Royal Academy in 1830.[13] Five years later, when the infirm Soane was awarded a Gold medal by the 'Architects of England', Chantrey's bust stood for him at the celebrations, decked with a garland and accompanied by busts of Vitruvuis, Palladio, Michelangelo, Inigo Jones and Wren. Then, after Soane's death and in accordance with his wishes, the marble was set in its present position, displacing a bust of Napoleon, flanked by images of Raphael and Michelangelo and below a bust of the painter Lawrence.[14]

Coming Face to Face

From the examples discussed so far it would seem that the settings in which busts are placed and the sequences of which they form part help to determine their meaning and prompt certain interpretations on the part of the viewer. But at the same time, the portrait bust might claim to be one of the most self-sufficient or, at least, self-contained of images. While the relatively restricted range of conventions employed and the apparent 'sameness' of busts allow them to be readily accommodated as collective groups within architectural spaces, the primary perceptual relationship is not between the image of the sitter and the setting but between the sitter and the individual viewer. However much part of a larger group or ensemble a particular bust might be, the viewer perceives it most effectively by coming face to face. The artificial nature of the bust as a fragment – a truncated part of the body – is a register of the way we see the head and shoulders of a person only as we come close. It is this – along with its existence in the spectator's space as a three-dimensional image – that can make such an artificial form seem so real.

Not all busts, of course, were executed to be viewed face to face. Those colossal marble images – whether Chantrey's busts of Nelson and his admirals at Greenwich or Harriet Hosmer's statue of Senator Benson – that became popular in the early nineteenth century were intended to tower above the viewer.[15] (In the latter case one fictional viewer evidently took the statue's size too literally for when Tom Sawyer saw 'the greatest man in the world' one Fourth of July, 'Mr Benson, an actual United States senator, proved an overwhelming disappointment – for he was not twenty-five feet high or anywhere in the neighbourhood of it.'[16] Much smaller busts could also be distanced from the spectator by being set in the pediment of a bookcase or above a doorway, as appears to have been the case with the version of Roubiliac's *Pope* that belonged to the Earl of Mansfield (FIG.6). However, other versions of this same bust, along with many marble portraits by eighteenth-century sculptors such as Roubiliac and Houdon (FIG.7), were subtly finished in such a way that predicated close and attentive viewing of their surfaces. Just this mode of close viewing, already perhaps assumed in some of Bernini's busts, encouraged the viewer to come closer to the sitter and so, in the imagination, engage in equal dialogue.

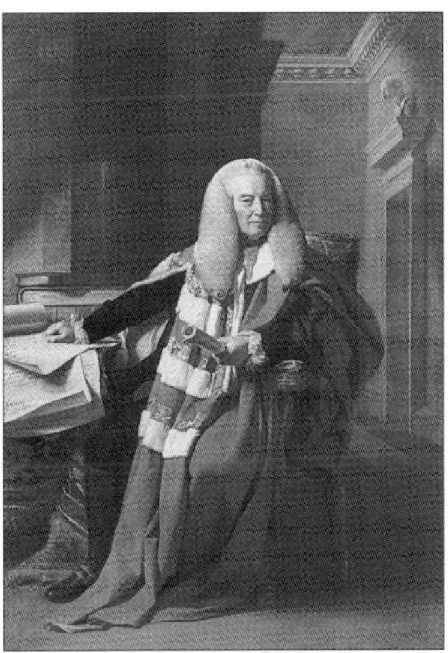

Fig.6 John Singleton Copley (1738–1815)
William Murray, 1ˢᵗ Earl of Mansfield
*c.*1783 Oil on Canvas
By courtesy of the National Portrait
Gallery, London

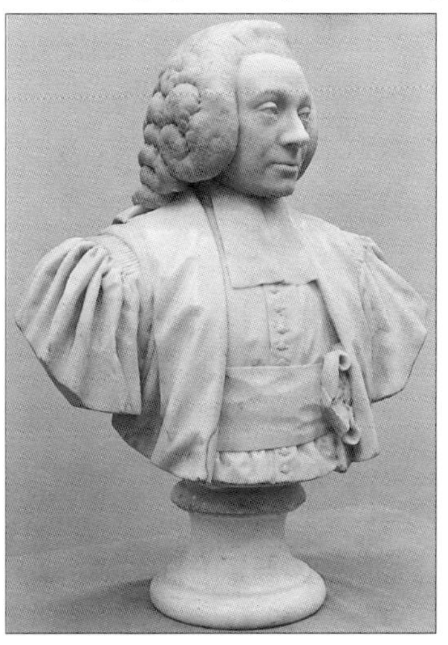

Fig.7 Jean-Antoine Houdon (1741–1828)
**Armand-Thomas Hue,
Marquis de Miromesnil**
1775 Marble
Victoria & Albert Museum, London

Even when busts might be arranged together to represent a collective identity and a set of shared beliefs, as in the Temple of Friendship at Stowe, this mode of engagement is not excluded. Indeed, as the building in which they are set was probably used by many of the very people represented, it is likely that a sitter in contemporary dress would have been seen by some of his fellows looking at his own image in classical dress. Perhaps the apparent solemnity of the marble bust and the contemporary literature that was produced to explicate the meanings of the gardens and sculpture at Stowe have occluded the element of parody and humour that may have been involved in the viewing of such works. Coming face to face in this manner was certainly assumed to be a familiar way of approaching the portrait bust by Daumier when he confronted the profile of a (bespectacled) sitter/patron/viewer with his (unbespectacled) marble bust at an exhibition (FIG.8). As Richard Brilliant has pointed out, the visual joke lies in the confrontation and comparison of the two profiles, apparent to us, but not to the complaining patron. But if Daumier's representation plays on this fiction, it also makes an assumption about the viewing of busts in such a context. Here setting and viewing do not involve a bust being lined up with others or placed in an architectural context, instead the sculptural portrait is brought into direct spatial relationship with the viewer. Such a setting does not distance the individual likeness, merging it with others, but, on the contrary, draws attention to the specificity and idiosyncracies of a sitter's features.

When bust and setting are considered in this way, the truncation – the line cutting off the image – takes on new significance and potential. The truncation indicates not only where the image ends but also the point where the spectator's space borders that of the sitter. A liminal zone, it marks the boundary where the setting begins. Some of the conventions formulated by sculptors for truncations in part mask the brutal severing of the torso but others function as a device that negotiates between the space of the viewer and that of the sitter, between the setting and the image. The distinctiveness of many busts lies not simply in the specific features of individual physiognomies but in the treatment of truncation and socle, the base on which the bust is placed. Coming face to face involves more than faces. Consequently, the direct engagement of the viewer with the representation of the sitter in the way I have described underpins and to some degree determines the choice of particular conventions and formats. In the case of Lemoyne's bust of the painter Coypel, for example, the sitter turns his head dramatically to his left, while drapery swirls down from his shoulder, across the concave back, and over the base of the socle (FIG.9). By treating the truncation – the borderline between viewer's and sitter's space – in this idiosyncratic way, the sculptor puts into question whether there is any front view and leaves us uncertain as to the angle from which we might approach the sitter. The sculpture's 'arc of address' – to borrow Michael Baxandall's phrase – is at the same time widened and rendered ambiguous.[17] Here, then, the treatment of the truncation and the socle to some degree establishes and controls the setting. There is no way in which Coypel's bust would be lost in the sculptural crowd, thanks to the strategy employed by Lemoyne to shift the familiar dynamic between sitter and viewer, as well as, at least implicitly, that between bust and setting.

Taking One's Place, Leaving One's Mark

Coming face to face is not a static experience and both viewers and settings change. We might perhaps imagine the ageing Cobham and his friends looking wryly at their own marble (and younger) images in the Temple of Friendship. The most significant of these changes was, of course, the death of the sitter. At this point the memorialising potential

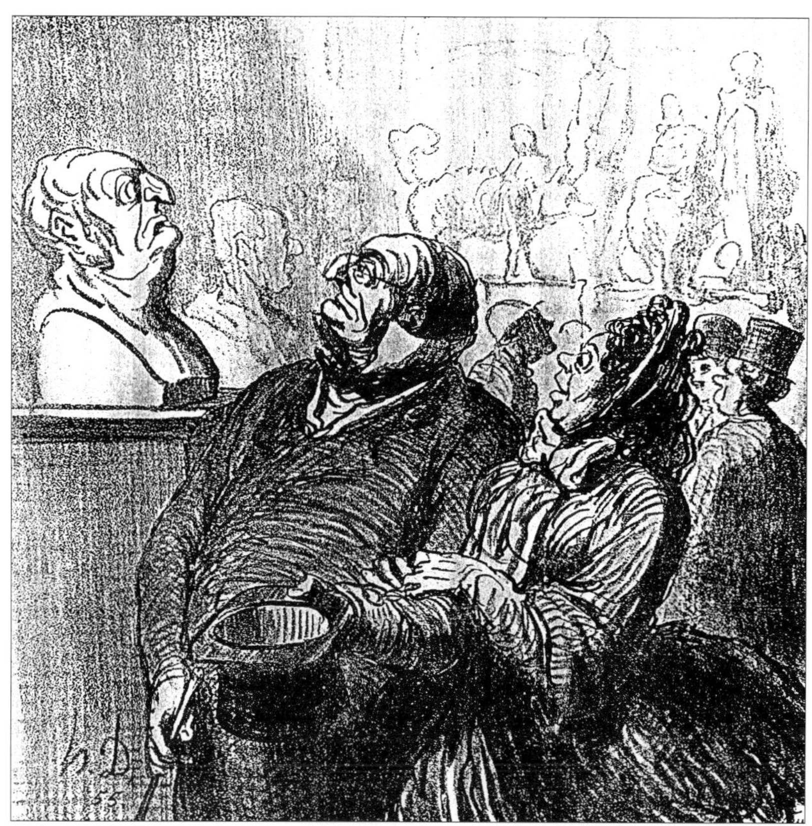

Fig.8 Honoré Daumier (1808–1879)
There's No Doubt About It …
from **The Public at the Exhibition**
1864 Lithograph

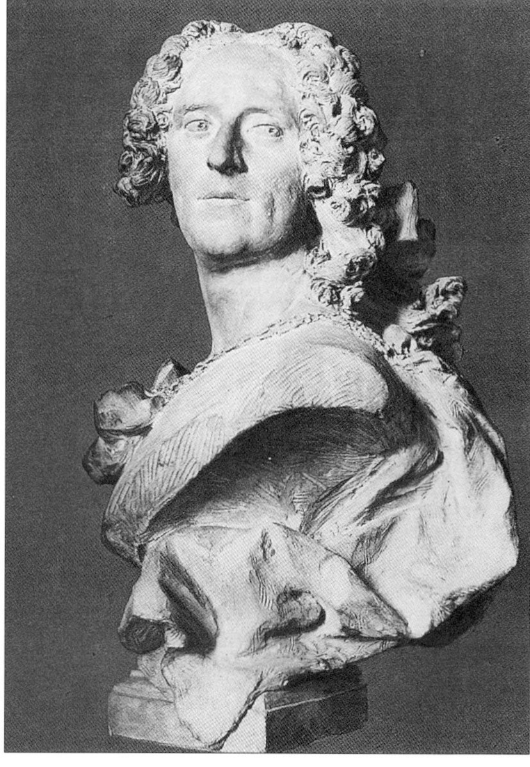

Fig.9 Jean-Baptiste Lemoyne (1704–1778)
Noël-Nicolas Coypel
1730 Terracotta
Musée du Louvre, Paris

that had remained only implicit while the bust represented a living contemporary was effectively realised. And it was this change from living to dead that would often prompt alterations to a bust's setting, as we have already seen in the case of Soane. Just such a shift in viewing conditions may be followed by means of the evidence available about another celebrated Chantrey bust, the marble of Sir Walter Scott. The bust was not commissioned but carried out in 1822 on the initiative of the sculptor who then (in Scott's own words) 'made Lady Scott a present of the fine bust he cut of my poor noddle three years ago.'[18] It took several years to reach Abbotsford and its setting there was a matter of some debate. As Scott wrote, 'There is only one capital place in the House & that is at the far end of the library. But it is already occupied by a cast of Shakespeare's tomb and bust from Stratford upon Avon and I cannot think of dispossessing them for a successor so unworthy.' On its arrival in 1828 the bust was apparently displayed on the 'plain white side-table of the purest marble' envisaged for it four years before, but on Scott's death his son replaced the Shakespeare sculpture with the bust of his father, so giving the author's image pride of place as well as making the library, and indeed the whole house, a memorial to the writer who created it (FIG.10).

The marble at Abbotsford was not the only version of Chantrey's portrait and settings other than the writer's house existed. One version (after, rather than by, Chantrey) was set up in Westminster Abbey, close to but not in Poets' Corner. Here it joined a multitude of monuments which to Henry James seemed 'not only local but social – a sort of corporate company … a company in possession, with a high standard of distinction, of immortality'.[19] Scott's bust is placed on a bracket and at first sight seems to jostle rather uncomfortably with the figure of Eloquence on Roubiliac's monument to an earlier Scot, the 2nd Duke of Argyll (FIG.11). But if we take a lead from James' observation that these images of different dates 'seem, with their converging faces, to scrutinise decorously the claims of each new recumbent glory', we might see Scott's bust through its setting continuing (and giving new life to) an earlier tradition of rhetoric as well as exemplifying Scottish genius in another form. Yet another context for a version of Chantrey's Scott is found along the road from the Scottish National Portrait Gallery where, on the corner of Castle Street and Queen Street, a pawnbroker has its windows topped by various ornaments including the bust (FIG.12). But by now the bust – albeit a debased copy – is rendered largely invisible through being part of a miscellaneous group that decorates rather than commemorates.

In this example, the portrait bust seems to have become a marginal and largely worthless mode of sculptural representation. The classicising format that had been explored tentatively and edgily as something quite new in Rysbrack's *Nottingham* marble had by this point become so familiar and overworked that it became difficult for viewers to see such images as anything other than standardised and boring. When numerous busts such as

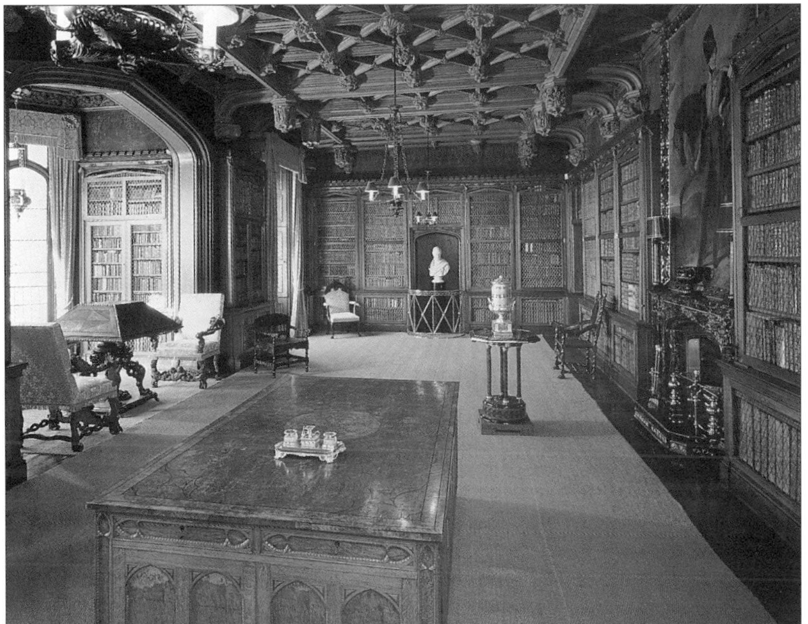

Fig.10

Figs. 10–12 Sir Francis Leggatt Chantrey
(1781–1841)
Sir Walter Scott
1822 Marble
The Library at Abbotsford House,
Roxburghshire (Fig.10)
Westminster Abbey, London (Fig.11)
Castle Street and Queen Street,
Edinburgh (Fig.12)

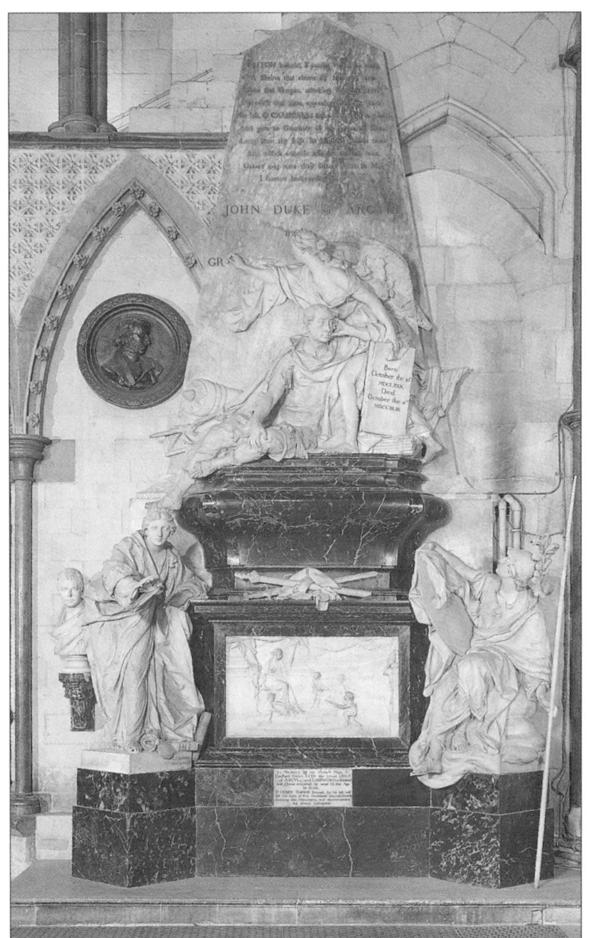

Fig.11

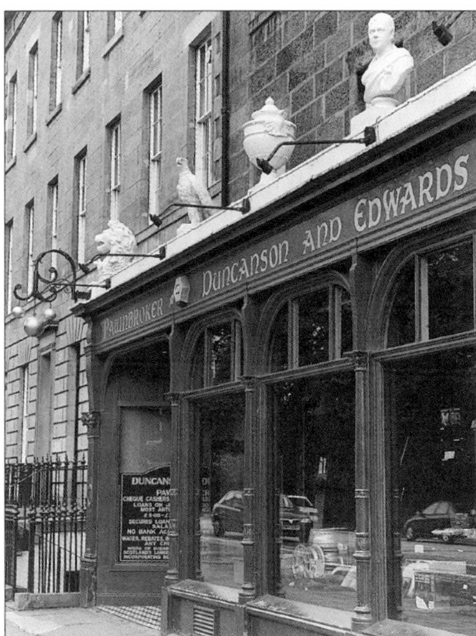

Fig.12

these were set up in regular lines so that they no longer animated a setting but merged into it, other strategies had to be adopted by sculptors and their patrons. One of these was to follow Lemoyne's example and play with the conventions of the bust form – especially the truncation – so that busts might belong but also stand out. This seems to have been an option adopted for many of the images in this exhibition. While they all might at first sight seem to be examples of the same type, each of them exploits some feature that allows it to stand out from its fellows and its setting. An individual might have joined the club, but viewer and sitter could still be encouraged to come face to face.

Approaching the portrait bust in the ways outlined here involves engaging not only with individual likeness, but also with the setting. And, by taking account of the settings in which busts were placed, we can perhaps think rather differently about conventions and their meanings. Given the importance of the contexts for such images, it is unlikely that a patron, setting out to commission a bust, would not have imagined where it might be placed. Incorporation into a family sequence or some other extended group could have a bearing on the convention adopted by sitter and sculptor. Take the case of Richard Hurd, later Bishop of Worcester, who described to Sir Edward Littleton in March 1753 how he had visited Rysbrack to discuss sitting for his bust:

> When I called upon him he said it would be necessary to sit three or four times and that it would take up eight or ten days.…He seems to think my bad head would not be disgraced by being turned into stone. And we have almost agreed about the attitude and dress. The head is to turn a little on one side, no cap or wig, but a thin hair upon it – a little loose drapery over the shoulders.[20]

We have no evidence about where this bust was to be situated, but perhaps the classicising mode Hurd selected was seen as more appropriate to a particular setting. The same might have also applied to the choice made by the musicologist Dr Charles Burney who opted not for Roman dress but for academic robes when he sat to Nollekens. This was not, however, without its problems, for, having borrowed a gown and hood, both he and the sculptor 'were such noodles we cd not put them on'.[21] In the event, Burney regarded the result as his 'most magnificent representative', suggesting mockingly that 'I shall become a very Narcissus & pine myself into a daffodil'. In each of these two instances, we see an image being formulated by patron and sculptor, with a concern for individual likeness and the way in which this was to be framed. Yet, at the same time, their sculptural portraits no doubt expected company and were not designed to be seen alone. Perhaps by taking account of the company they kept, we might also glimpse again the individuality of the portrait bust, allowing each 'magnificent representative' a return to life.

Malcolm Baker

NOTES

1. The individual busts are described in W. Lefanu, *A Catalogue of the Portraits and other Paintings Drawings and Sculpture in the Royal College of Surgeons of England*, Edinburgh and London, 1960

2. *A New Description of Sir John Soane's Museum*, London, 1955 and successive editions, provide a detailed account of the building and its contents.

3. 'Detached Thoughts (October 15 1821–May 18 1822)' in L. A. Marchand ed., *Byron's Letters and Journals*, vol. 5, London, 1864, p.21.

4. Henry St. John, Viscount Bolinbroke, *Letters on the Study and Use of History*, 1749.

5. My account of the relationship between the busts of Cocchi and Huntingdon is based on letters and inventories among the Hastings papers in the Henry H. Huntington Library, San Marino, California; these are mainly to be found in HA 1528, HA 1529 and HA Inventories Box 3, Folder A.

6. Their setting is discussed in M. Baker, *Figured in Marble. The Making and Viewing of Eighteenth-century Sculpture*, London and Los Angeles, 2000, chapt. 4.

7. J. Kenworthy-Browne, 'The Temple of Liberty at Woburn Abbey', *Apollo*, 130 (1989), pp. 27–32.

8. C. Avery, 'Neo-Classical Portraits by Pistucci and Rauch', in *Studies in European Sculpture*, London, 1981, pp. 253–60; J. von Simson, *Christian Daniel Rauch*, Berlin, 1996, pp. 94, 181, 234–5.

9. R. A. Kinglake, *Somerset Worthies*, London and Taunton, 1891; A. Dobson, 'The Taunton Bust of Fielding', *The Magazine of Art*, July 1883, pp. 371–4. I am grateful to Julie Allen, Barbara Baker and Mary Baker for investigating the present settings of these busts that are still in the Shire Hall.

10. *Baedecker's Guide to Great Britain*, 1906.

11. James uses the phrase about Browning. H. James, 'Browning in Westminster Abbey', in *English Hours*, London, 1960 (first published, 1905), p.34.

12. The bust is described in an inventory of Burley dated 1772–4 (Leicestershire Record Office DG 7, Box XXII, Inv. 4) as having belonged to 'the Honble William Finch and was removed from his house in Savile Row where it stood in his Lifetime'.

13. For Soane's bust see A. Yarrington *et al.*, 'An Edition of the Ledger of Sir Francis Chantrey', *Walpole Society*, 56 (1991/1992), pp. 250–51.

14. G. Darley, *John Soane. An Accidental Romantic*, New Haven and London, 1999, pp. 275, 316

15. For Chantrey's busts see Yarrington *et al.*, p. 21; for a photo of Harriet Hosmer alongside her colossal statue of Benson, see M. Kemp ed., *The Oxford History of Western Art*, Oxford, 1999, p. 344.

16. M. Twain, *The Adventures of Tom Sawyer*, 1876, chapt. 22. Daumier print is discussed by Richard Brilliant, *Portraiture*, London, 1991, pp. 59–62.

17. M. Baxandall, *The Limewood Sculptors of Renaissance Germany*, New Haven and London, 1980, p. 166.

18. On Scott's bust and its settings see Alex Potts's entry in Yarrington *et al.*, pp. 136–7 and C. Wainwright, *The Romantic Interior*, New Haven and London, 1989, pp. 184–5; 190–91.

19. James, *op cit.*, p.33.

20. Letters to Sir Edward Littleton, Staffordshire Record Office, MS D1413/1.

21. R. Lonsdale, *Dr Charles Burney. A literary biography*, Oxford, 1965, pp. 415, 418.

BUSTS AND IDENTITY

OF ALL THE many forms of portraiture the sculpted bust is at the same time the most artificial and the most real, but it is probably its artificiality which is most striking to the modern spectator. Although a handful of coloured terracotta busts have been present since the Renaissance and coloured, if not naturalistic, forms have been used to great effect in recent times, the traditional colour of the bust is monochrome: the white of plaster or marble and the brown or black of unpainted terracotta or patinated bronze. These traditional colours depend upon the materials of sculpture, and the materials in their turn depend on function. Bust sculpture was, from ancient times, first and foremost the memorial form of the portrait; it often appeared on tombs and, where it did not, it was usually the form used to perpetuate the memory of a figure whose reputation was expected to last at least as long as his (or, rarely, her) durable effigy. By far the majority of busts were of famous people, and there is a particular poignancy in the fact that, wrested from their original contexts and gathered into museums, so many of these lively and individual images (e.g. exhibits 4 and 22) have lost their identities, and sometimes the identity of those who made them as well.

The celebrity of most subjects of busts also meant that they were often manufactured in substantial quantities. Joseph Nollekens, the most prolific English bust specialist of the late eighteenth century, supplied around thirty marble replicas of his portrait of the Whig politician *Charles James Fox* (5), and more than twice as many of Fox's great rival, William Pitt the Younger, as well as some six hundred copies in plaster.[1] An English traveller in Rome in 1817 noted that, because sculpture was so cheap there, plaster casts of busts of King George III, Fox, Pitt, Nelson and others were shipped from London to be copied in marble, and sent back to England at a total cost of £22 each.[2] Nollekens had very little part in the carving of his marbles, not to mention the casting of the plasters, although this seems to have been a source of surprise to Fox himself. The sculptor reported to the painter and diarist Joseph Farington in 1803:

> that Fox was very ignorant abt. Sculpture. While Nollekens was making a Model in Clay of his
> Bust, after he had sat 6 or 7 times He asked Nollekens why he did not execute it in marble instead

of Clay. Nollekens shewed him that while working in Clay He could alter every part as it might be required but that could not be done in Marble; whatever was chipped off could not be restored.[3]

The sculptor's hand, after making the initial clay model, would be confined for the most part to the finishing touches to the marble which had been carved by studio assistants.

The mass-production of busts was only one factor which helped to make this the most artificial of portrait forms. Although there are no truly colossal and no miniature busts in this exhibition, the manipulation of scale has always been an important feature of portrait sculpture, as a vehicle of respect or intimacy, and as an aid to the spectators' imagination.[4] The imagination is also powerfully stimulated by the fragment, and the bust is, above all, a fragment of the body. This sense of the incomplete is heightened in the more recent work where the head emerges from a naked and irregular chest, particularly marked in Derwent Wood's bronze of *Ambrose McEvoy* (12) or Albert Toft's *Robert Bontine Cunninghame Graham* (11). Epstein's version of *Cunninghame Graham* (28) adopts the even more unsettling convention of the decapitated head, which has in the twentieth century enjoyed a vogue comparable in scale to its opposite number, the half-length including chest and arms, here represented again brilliantly by Epstein (8) and especially by Frank Dobson's elegantly sprawling image of the actress *Margaret Rawlings* (9).

The half-length with arms derives from a Florentine Renaissance rather than a classical tradition; but another artificial convention which is extensively represented in this exhibition has a purely classical, indeed archaeological origin. The presentation of blind, blank eyes, those disturbingly alienating features which further remove the sculpted bust from the land of the living, derives from the mistaken idea that this was a classical practice. The misunderstanding arose from the discovery of ancient busts with blank eyes and from the long-standing reluctance to believe that they had originally been inlaid with gaudy coloured stones, or that the iris and pupil had been indicated with paints which had been erased by time. Blank eyes reinforced the notion of the inherent ideality of classical art and were a congenial prop to the prevailing classicising aesthetic of sculpture around 1800. But it will also be clear from this exhibition that there was no uniformity of approach to eyes, even in thoroughly classicising images. Joseph Wilton's very 'Roman' effigy of the elder *Pitt* (17) incises iris and pupil with great force, although the upcast glance conveys, it is true, an effect of distraction from the ordinary world of the spectator, while in Joseph Gott's *George Banks* (2) the engagingly mobile mouth is counteracted by the completely impenetrable sightless stare. Sir Francis Chantrey, whose busts of the politician *Francis Horner* and the engineer *John Rennie* (19, 16) both have blank eyes, took a characteristically pragmatic and individualising view. As he told a sitter a few years after these works were executed:

In the expression of some faces the eyes are the feature that takes the lead. When that is the case,

> I mark the pupils, when it is otherwise, I do not: and a very simple experiment always decides which should be done.[5]

Chantrey, alas, does not tell us what this simple experiment was.

So even in a period of Neo-Classicism and Romanticism, when 'Nature' was the leading aesthetic slogan, the sculpted bust was inevitably artificial, and this artificiality increased as the nineteenth century wore on and the status and independence of the artist increased. Marble was overtaken by bronze as the preferred medium of bust sculpture, and bronze, as a cast medium, could readily reproduce the individual impression of the artist's hand. As the busts of the novelist John Galsworthy demonstrate (25, 26), bronze is quite capable of imitating the smoothness and even something of the softness of marble; but Gaudier-Brzeska, for example, followed Picasso in constructing an image from Cubist facets (7), and Epstein, the great virtuoso of modelling, abandoned all pretence of imitating flesh, or hair, or cloth in the hand-made vigour of his rugged surfaces. At the opposite extreme of artifice, Dobson's *Sir Osbert Sitwell* (3), with its slicked-down, head-hugging helmet of hair, embodies the precision of the machine age, especially in its highly-polished and reflective brass versions, one of them now in the Tate Gallery. T. E. Lawrence (Lawrence of Arabia), who watched it being made over several days, called it 'the finest portrait bust of modern times.'[6]

Matters of Life and Death

If the empty eyes of many earlier busts were an accidental consequence of classicising aspirations, the palpable fleshiness of their surroundings, its creasing and sagging, its veins and warts and wrinkles, were no less a consequence of the 'realism' which was seen to characterise ancient Roman portraiture.[7] In comparison with the painted portrait, the sculpted bust is remarkable for its attention to the nuances of facial structure and to surface, and this was facilitated by several practices which seem to have been particularly common among portrait sculptors. One was the taking of life or death masks directly from the subject, and such masks were a common part of the visual culture of eighteenth- and nineteenth-century Europe. Just as libraries were a major setting for the display of busts (see Malcolm Baker in this volume and at note 8), so libraries often housed collections of the life or death masks of notable men. Thus in the 1830s the Cambridge University Library displayed masks of King Charles XII of Sweden, of the Cambridge hero Sir Isaac Newton, and of Pitt and Fox and other politicians, a collection of which there is now no trace.[8] Nollekens was particularly anxious to make his busts on the basis of authentic sources. His biographer, J. T. Smith, described his practice:

Nollekens, after reading of the death of any great person in the newspaper, generally ordered some plaster to be got ready, so that he might attend at a minute's notice. One day, when a lady who had sent for him desired him not to make so free with her dear husband's corpse, he observed, 'Oh, bless ye, you had better let me close his eye-lids; for then, when I cast him in my mould, he'll look for all the world as if he was asleep. Why do you take on so? You do wrong to *prey* upon such a dismal prospect; do leave the room to me and my man; I am used to it, it makes no impression on me; I have got a good many noted down in my journal.'

Mr Sebastian Gahagan, the Sculptor, Mr Nollekens's assistant, attended him to cast the face of Lord Lake, after his decease; his Lordship's brother was then inconsolably pacing the room, but Mr Nollekens shook him by the elbow, and applied to him for a little sweet-oil, a large basin, some water, and pen, ink, and paper.

The gentleman, astonished at this want of decency, referred him to the servant; and Nollekens, after he had taken the mask, muttered the following soliloquy: 'Now, let me see, I must begin to measure him; where's my callipers? I must take him from his chin to the upper pinnacle of the head; I'll put him down in ink; ay, that will do; now, I must have him from his nose to the back part of his skull; well, now let's take his shoulders; now for his neck; well, now I've got him all.'[9]

But Nollekens was also among the many portraitists who found death-masks disappointingly deceptive. Farington reported in September 1806 how the sculptor:

> shewed me a cast which he took from the face of *Mr Fox* as he lay in his coffin, two or three nights ago. – Dr Vaughan, He said, called upon Him on the morning of that day & proposed to Him to take a *cast*, saying that an opportunity ought not to be lost in the instance of so great a man. – Nollekens replied, that probably there was so great a change from what Mr Fox appeared when living & well that it wd. not be like Him. – Dr Vaughan assured him that was not the case. – Nollekens accordingly went at 9 o'clock that night to Chiswick, & now told me the alteration was so great that he should not have known it to be Mr Fox. – He took a Cast, and I was surprised indeed at the alteration, for it appeared to me to have no resemblance to Him, but to be in feature and in general form another kind of face. – Nollekens having measured Mr Fox's head when he made the admirable well-known Bust of Him, compared the dimensions with those of the cast & found that in the width from ear to ear the face had shrunk an Inch and a half, & other parts in proportion.[10]

It is in fact rather surprising that Nollekens should have laid such emphasis on death-masks, for in them, as we have seen (32), the eyes are invariably closed and the features frozen; yet his biographer Smith remarked – and the liveliness of his best busts demonstrates – that he was apt to base his likenesses on the movable parts of the face, the eyes, mouth and nose, rather than on bone-structure. The 'low and rugged brow', said Smith, which Nollekens gave to Fox in his bust (5) was in contrast to the 'even, high and promi-nent' brow of the mask, 'full of dignified grandeur.'[11]

Early in the nineteenth century, new developments in the mechanics of drawing made the urge for an objective starting-point for bust-portraits easier to satisfy. In 1806 the scientist William Hyde Wollaston patented the *camera lucida*, a small portable device using a prism as a lens to project a virtual image on to a sheet of paper. Wollaston was a close friend of Chantrey, who made his bust, and Chantrey came to use the device to make pre-cise preliminary drawings of his subjects in the most economical way. But, as in the case of

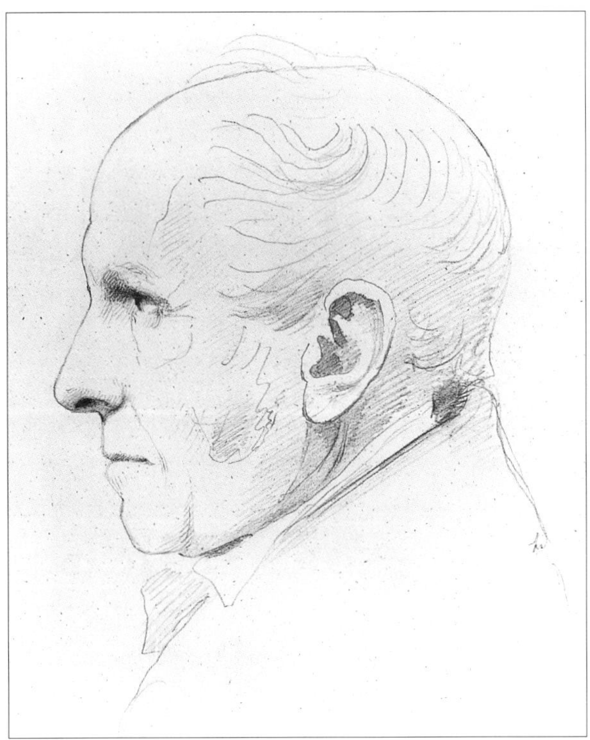

Fig.1 Sir Francis Leggatt Chantrey
(1781–1841)
James Dunlop
Camera lucida drawing
1836
By courtesy of the
National Portrait Gallery, London

the masks, it was only the structure and proportions of the head which could be established by this means, and Chantrey, even more than Nollekens, laid great emphasis on the mobility of the features to give life to his images. In 1836 the American painter C. R. Leslie witnessed how the sculptor made these preparatory drawings for a bust of James Dunlop (FIG.1):

> Mr Dunlop had been sitting to Chantrey, who fixed the back of his head in a wooden machine to keep him perfectly still, and then drew with a camera lucida the profile and front face of the size of life. He afterwards gave a little light and shade to the drawings, and said 'I shall not require you to sit still after this'. He said, 'I always determine in my mind the expression to be given; and unless I can see the face distinctly, and with that expression when I close my eyes, I can do nothing. If I can, I can often make the face more like in the absence of the sitter than in the presence.'[12]

Reading the Head

J. T. Smith urged the students of Nollekens' portrait of Fox to check out that mask in one of the several collections of casts and skulls which were an indication that bust portraiture was becoming an important adjunct to the study of personality in the Romantic period. The ancient study of physiognomics, the reading of character from the external features of the body, gained a new dimension in the eighteenth century with Johann Caspar Lavater's highly-influential attempt to remove the science from the realm of abstraction and link it closely to the portraits of well-known figures of the past and the present. Although the first image in the richly-illustrated English edition of Lavater's *Essays on Physiognomy* shows the author contemplating a sculpted bust, sculpture played a very limited role in this study, which relied much more on the newly-popular medium of the profile silhouette for the crucial analysis of the salient features of forehead, nose and chin. One illustration, however, from an unattributed sculpted effigy of the English philosopher John Locke, although entitled 'defective copies of a very middling bust', is nonetheless seen to have Locke's 'essential and fundamental character'[13] (FIG.2).

Although a number of painters, and, especially, engravers subscribed to Lavater's English edition, there do not appear to be any sculptors on the list, and it was only a generation later that a new phase in physiognomical analysis, phrenology, brought the three-dimensional portrait onto centre-stage. The analysis of the mind into more than thirty discrete 'faculties' and their location in specific parts of the brain had been developed by the German physician Franz Joseph Gall in the 1790s, and popularised in England and Scotland by his publicist Johann Caspar Spurzheim in the 1810s. The importance of these ideas for portrait-sculpture was, of course, that the balance of faculties in any individual subject could be read from the relative sizes of those parts of the brain which incorporated them, and this, in turn, was manifested on the surface of the cranium in the form of protuberances or bumps. Just as a sculptor such as Nollekens had been used to taking his callipers to measure the proportions of the head of a corpse, so a subject's bumps could now be measured with a device such as George Combe's *Craniometer* (FIG.3). The museum of heads to which Smith directed his readers belonged to James De Ville, at 367 The Strand, in London. DeVille, a cast-maker by profession, had learned of Gall and Spurzheim in 1821 and, before the decade was out, had assembled a collection of some eighteen hundred casts and human skulls, as well as three to four thousand animal skulls for comparison. He had also developed a substantial practice as a phrenologist, a lecturer on phrenology and a consultant in cases of insanity.[14] The first life-mask taken by DeVille with a phrenological purpose was apparently that of the poet, painter and visionary William Blake (FIG.4), which he felt would be 'representative of the imaginative faculty'.[15] Much of the popularity of death masks derived from their sensational character – comparable perhaps to Marc

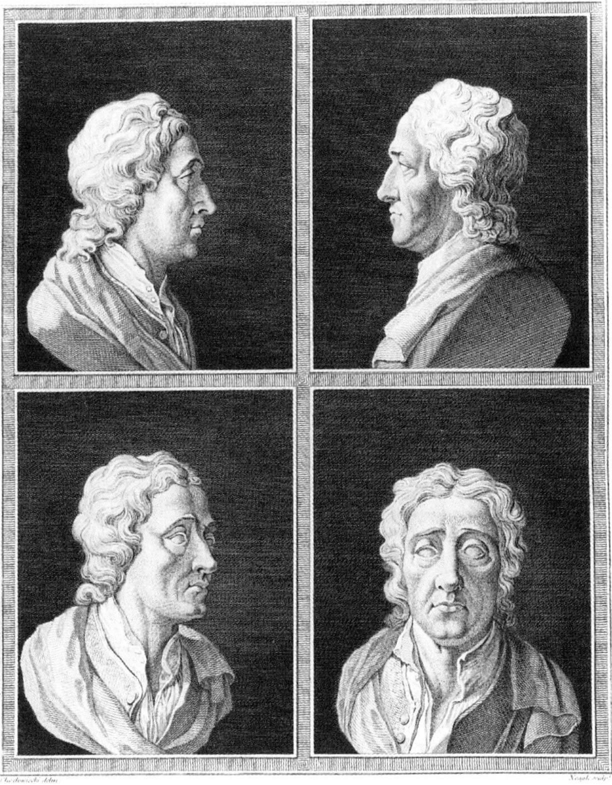

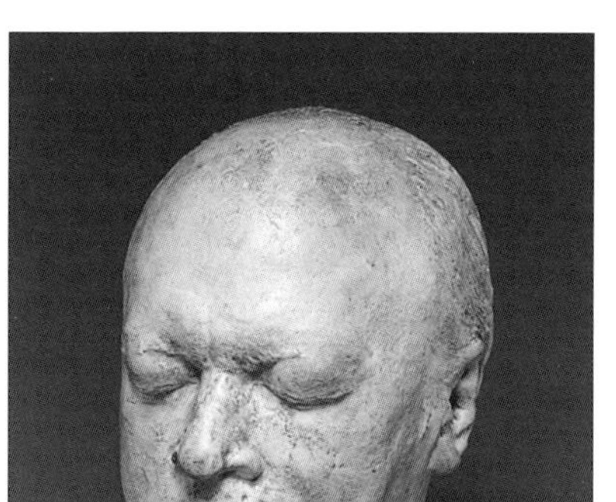

Fig.2 Johann Kaspar Lavater (1741–1801)
Four Views of a Bust of John Locke
Engraving
By permission of the British Library, London

Fig.4 James DeVille
Life Mask of William Blake
*c.*1823 Plaster
Fitzwilliam Museum, University of Cambridge

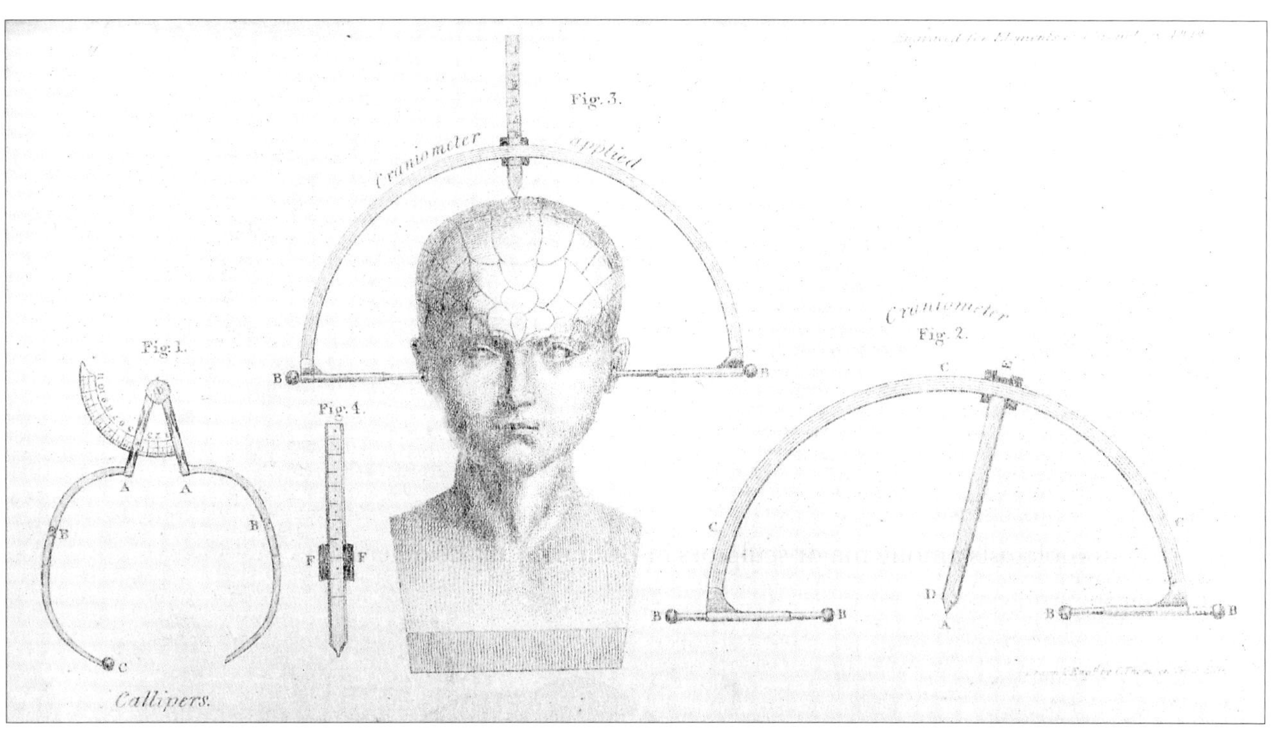

Fig.3 George Combe (1788–1858)
Illustration of a Craniometer
By permission of the British Library, London

Quinn's *Self*, the bust of his frozen blood shown at the Royal Academy *Sensation* exhibition in 1997 – for many were taken from executed criminals and formed part, as indeed did physiognomy itself, of the anxious search for a key to identifying the criminal type. Substantial collections of masks of this type still survive in Edinburgh (among other types) and Dundee, and at the Old Gaol in Melbourne, Australia. DeVille's museum inevitably included such a group of busts, which were noticed by Andrew Combe:

> In one division of the room, innumerable rows of criminal and vicious heads contrast in the magnitude of the base and occiput, and the shallowness of the coronal region, with the moderate base and well developed coronal region of the more moral and virtuous classes.[16]

But such disreputable subjects were unlikely to be commemorated in the more permanent form of sculpture.

For all his popularity, DeVille remained something of an amateur, and the capital of phrenology during the 1820s was not London but Edinburgh, home of the brothers George and Andrew Combe (30–33), who were very active propagandists for the science, and founders of the long-lived *Phrenological Journal*.[17] George Combe had been converted by Spurzheim's lectures in Edinburgh in the 1810s; his brother Andrew associated closely with Gall's propaganda as a medical student in Paris. Both brothers wrote extensively on phrenological subjects, but George devoted himself more exclusively to this, and, more important for us, to extending the scope of phrenology into the visual arts. In this he was assisted by the Edinburgh sculptor Lawrence Macdonald, the author of Andrew's bust (31), and whom George helped to make a definitive move to Rome in 1832. George met Macdonald there in the following decade and was stimulated to write an article on 'The application of phrenology to the fine arts' for the *Phrenological Journal* in 1844, the first of a series of essays which were later gathered into a book. Macdonald agreed that:

> It is as difficult to model a head with accuracy when one does not understand the mental qualities connected with the different parts of the brain, as to model an arm correctly in ignorance of its anatomy and motions.[18]

The early membership of the Phrenological society of Edinburgh included only one sculptor, Samuel Joseph (10, 13, 21), among its seven artists, and it would be difficult to find dedicated phrenologists among major sculptors in Britain.[19] On the other hand, the phrenologists themselves were not above turning to the evidence of sculpted busts in support of their theories. Gall's collection, for example, included a number of pre-phrenological unattributed busts of the philosopher Voltaire and the composer Gluck, as well as a plaster of the poet Goethe which, however, was criticised for its unnatural exaggeration of the organs of Pride and Vanity.[20]

This close relationship between phrenologists and bust sculptors is not at all surprising, for well before the arrival of the new science, sculptors had often sought to expose as far as possible the underlying structure of their subjects' heads. This exhibition includes no bewigged figures, and although this may clearly be linked to the dominantly classical associations of the bust form, there is in fact no shortage of eighteenth-century portrait busts which feature wigs. Yet it is true that even in the first half of the century Roubiliac

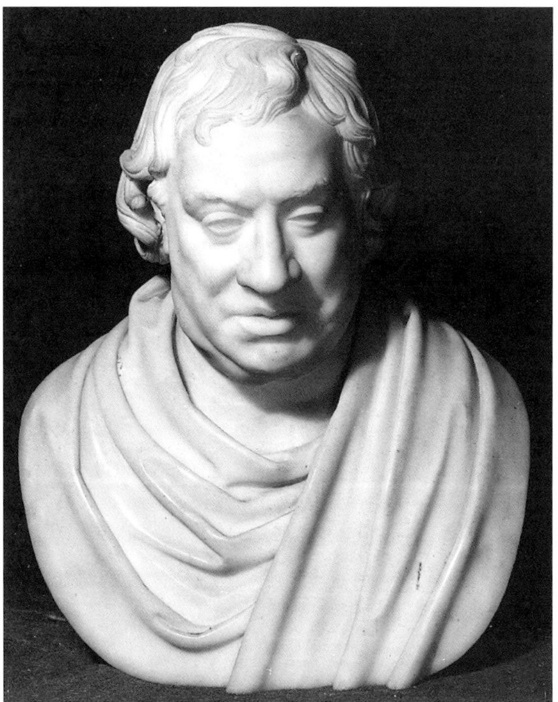

Fig.5 Joseph Nollekens (1737–1823)
Monument to Samuel Johnson
1777 Marble
Westminster Abbey, London

(c.1705–62), for example, avoided wigs when he could, and so did Nollekens, although he was not above modelling the abundant hair on Dr Johnson's bust in Westminster Abbey (FIG.5) from 'the flowing locks of a sturdy Irish beggar, originally a street paviour'.[21]

The sculptor argued, against the objections of his subject, that Johnson should properly have the appearance of an ancient poet, although the most famous poet of antiquity, Homer, as represented, for example, in Lavater's *Essays*, traditionally showed a rather bald head and a bushy beard. Beards were a great rarity in upper-class Europe in the eighteenth century; Nollekens modelled George III immediately after he had shaved,[22] and Fox's five-o'clock shadow, so congenial to the caricaturists, never appears on his smooth-cheeked busts (5) or even in painted portraits. But after 1800 fashions changed; in the late 1820s Chantrey had to pursuade the Duke of Sussex to shave off his whiskers before being modelled,[23] and the widespread wearing of facial hair during the Victorian and Edwardian periods meant that (although versions of Lavater's works continued to appear) the analysis of the whole face by physiognomists became nearly impossible.

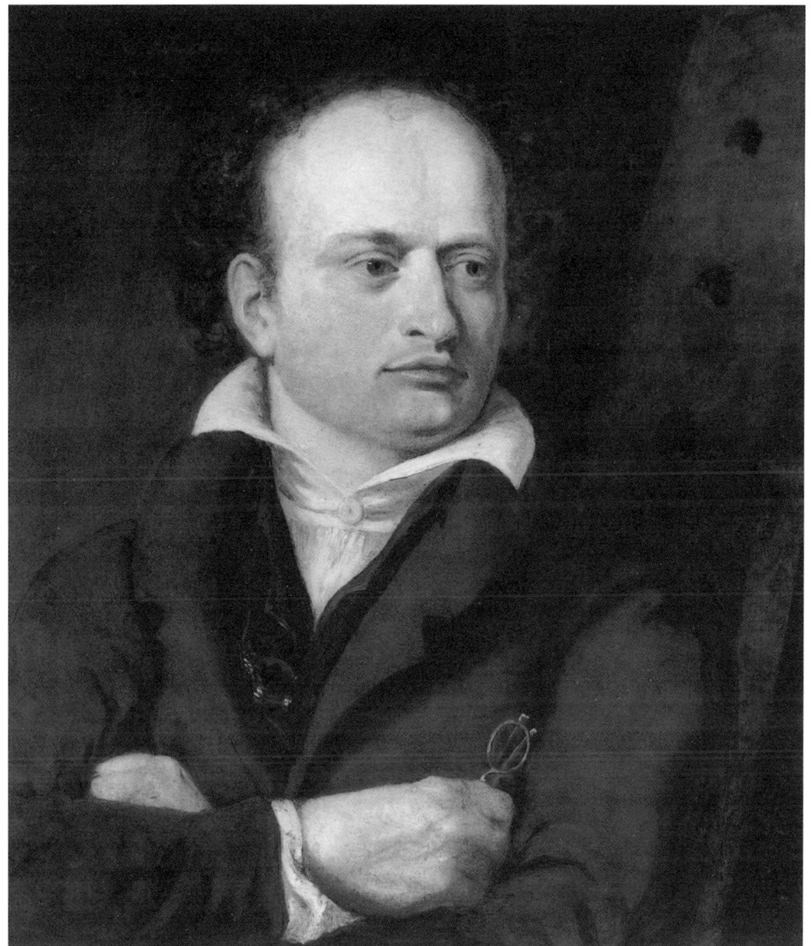

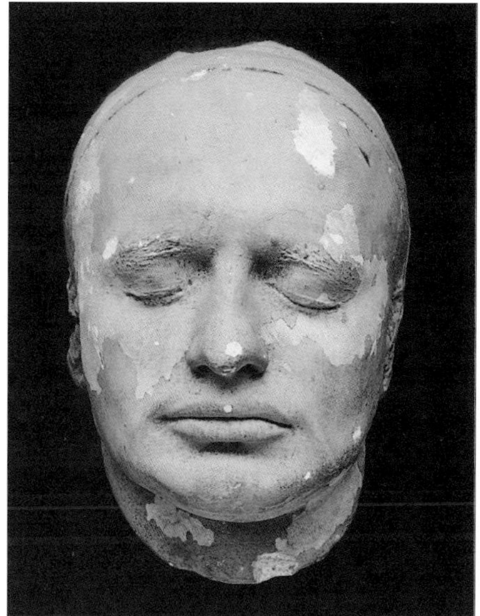

Fig.7 Unknown Artist
(Johann Gaspar Spurzheim 1776–1832?)
Life Mask of Benjamin Robert Haydon
*c.*1820 Plaster
By courtesy of the National Portrait Gallery,
London

Fig.6 Georgiana Margaretta Zornlin (1800–1881)
Benjamin Robert Haydon
1825
By courtesy of the National Portrait Gallery, London

As a sort of compensation, the new vogue for baldness in men offered fresh opportunities for phrenological study, and when, in 1825, the historical painter Benjamin Robert Haydon met Spurzheim at a London *soirée*, the phrenologist – as Haydon reported to Mary Mitford – complimented him on his baldness: 'Vy, your organs are more parfaite den eaver. How luckee you lose your hair.'[24] Haydon's enormous expanse of brow (FIG.6) was clearly an important part of his self-image as a genius; he had attended Spurzheim's lectures since 1815, the phrenologist made a life-mask of him (FIG.7), and Haydon introduced phrenology, somewhat tentatively, into the *Lectures on Painting and Design* which he gave in the 1840s.[25]

In the patriarchal society of Victorian England women were generally excluded from these phrenological speculations, just as they appear relatively rarely as a subject for busts. Yet the centre-parting and the smoothed-down hairstyle of the 1840s and 1850s (22) could, like the receding hairlines of their menfolk, open up the possibility of a phrenological study of the crown of the head for women as well. These demure and restrained styles were in marked contrast to the abundant flowing hair and large jaws of the Pre-Raphaelite women, which were to become such obvious signs of a bohemian style of life. Loose hair indicated loose morals.[26]

By the close of the nineteenth century phrenological analysis had gone the same way as classical associations in bust-portraiture, and the newer styles were characterised by an even greater mobility of pose and features. Yet a sculptor such as Epstein was still very much concerned with the underlying structure of the heads he modelled. The actor Emlyn Williams, who sat to him around 1930, remarked how Epstein circled round him and bent down 'to scrutinize a new plane of my face from another angle';[27] and the sculptor had to ask Einstein (FIG.8) to refrain from smoking his pipe during sittings because the smoke interfered with his clear view of the forms in that astonishing head.[28] The liveliness of Epstein's busts flows from the constantly moving reflections from the pitted surfaces and from the deeply-gouged eyes which, in sharp contrast to the 'classical' blank type, seem to give direct access, without benefit of any theory, to his subjects' minds.

Thus the portrait bust, despite a range of pose and context rather narrower than that of the painted portrait, was, and is, every bit as able to convey both a vivid individual presence and the dynamic of sculptural styles over the past two hundred years. Seen from below, as busts were so often seen in the eighteenth century, it could inspire respect and even awe, in tune with its marble distance. Seen on a level with the viewer, as we usually encounter the modern bronze bust in a museum or gallery, or some other public institution, we can inspect it from all angles and feel that the liveliness of the worked surface and the mobility of the deeply shadowed eyes give us access to the life of the subject. Above all, the bust reminds us that, for all the modern development of fingerprints and DNA profiles, it is the head alone that, in the social world, proclaims our identity.

John Gage

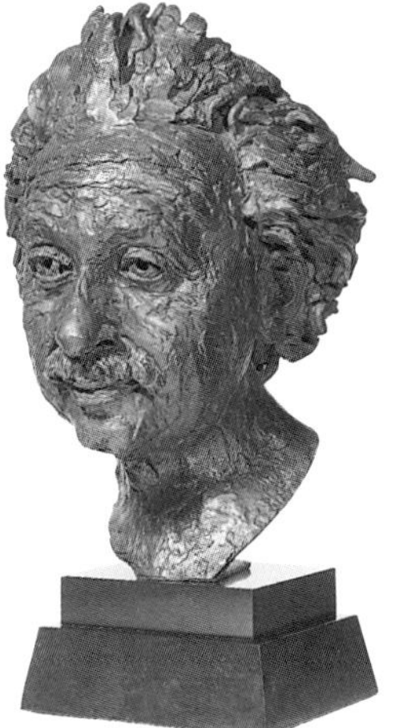

Fig.8 Sir Jacob Epstein (1880–1959)
Albert Einstein
1933 Bronze
Fitzwilliam Museum,
University of Cambridge

NOTES

1. K. Garlick, A. Macintyre, K. Cave (eds), *The Diary of Joseph Farington*, New Haven and London, 1978–84, 6 June 1807 (henceforward 'Farington'); J. T. Smith, *Nollekens and his Times*, (1828), London, 1949, 231–2 (henceforward 'Smith').

2. H. Matthews, *Diary of an Invalid*, London, 1822, I, 68. The sculptor was Lorenzo Bartolini; his price was less than one fifth of the going rate in England.

3. Farington, 18 August 1803. This was an amusing story of lay ignorance which circulated among artists for several years (see Farington 28 December 1806). But see also an anecdote in Smith, 176–7, which suggests that Nollekens did sometimes carve in the presence of his sitters.

4. The French Romantic sculptor P. J. David d'Angers, who made a speciality of the colossal portrait, was quite explicit about its poetic function (A. Bruel (ed.), *Les Carnets de David d'Angers*, Paris, 1958, I, 403).

5. A. Potts, *Sir Francis Chantrey, 1781–1841: Sculptor of the Great*, London, National Portrait Gallery, 1981, 8. Potts points out that Chantrey sometimes changed his mind when the clay model was transferred to marble.

6. O. Sitwell, *Laughter in the Next Room*, (1949), London, 1975, 186.

7. For the Roman 'realist' convention, J. D. Breckenridge, *Likeness: a conceptual History of Ancient Portraiture*, Evanston, 1968.

8. J. D. Passavant, *Tour of a German Artist in England*, (1836), London, 1978, II, 59–60. The display of busts in libraries has been discussed by M. Baker, 'The portrait sculpture' in D. McKitterick (ed.), *The Making of the Wren Library, Trinity College Cambridge*, Cambridge 1995, 110–37.

9. Smith, 229–30.

10. Farington, 19 September 1806.

11. Smith, 238.

12. C. R. Leslie, *Autobiographical Recollections* (1860), London, 1978, I, 152.

13. J. C. Lavater, *Essays on Physiognomy*, London, I, 1789, 255. For an introduction to Lavater's use of portraits, J. K. Stemmler, 'The physiognomical portraits of Johann Caspar Lavater', *Art Bulletin*, LXXV, 1993, 151–68.

14. A. C[ombe], 'Phrenology in London', *Phrenological Journal*, VI, 1829/30, 569–73. There is a short modern account of DeVille in D. de Giustino, *Conquest of the Mind: Phrenology and Victorian Social Thought*, London, 1975, 94–7.

15. D. Bindman (ed.), *William Blake: Catalogue of the Collection in the Fitzwilliam Museum, Cambridge*, Cambridge, 1970, 59. Blake's friend, George Richmond, who owned this bust, pointed to the distortion of the features due to the discomfort involved in making the mould.

16. Combe, loc. cit. 571. In 1840 the *Phrenological Journal* attacked the London shops selling plaster busts of notorious criminals for phrenological purposes, since they were 'either total or partial misrepresentations of nature' (T. M. Parssinen, 'Popular science and society: the phrenology movement in early Victorian Britain', *Journal of Social History*, VIII, 1974, 12).

17. See G. N. Cantor, 'The Edinburgh phrenology debate, 1803–1828', *Annals of Science*, 32, 1975, 195–218; S Shapin, 'Phrenological knowledge and social structure in early 19th century Edinburgh', ibid. 219–43; G. N. Cantor, 'A critique of Shapin's social interpretation of the Edinburgh phrenology debate', ibid. 245–56.

18. Combe, *Phrenology applied to Painting and Sculpture*, Edinburgh, 1855, 45. For Combe's close relationship with Macdonald, C. Gibbon, *The Life of George Combe*, London, 1878, I, 278, 288; II, 171–2. See also F. Pearson, 'Phrenology and Sculpture', *Leeds Arts Calendar*, 88, 1981 and T. Friedman in *Virtue and Vision: Sculpture and Scotland 1540–1990*, Edinburgh, National Gallery, 1991.

19. Though not in France, where David d'Angers was a devotee of the science (H. Jouin, *David d'Angers, sa Vie, ses Œuvres, ses Ecrits et ses Contemporaines*, Paris, 1878, 259, 342).

20. A. A. Royet, 'Catalogue, numerical and descriptive, of heads of men and animals, which composed the collection made by the late Dr Gall', *Phrenological Journal*, VI, 1829/30, 480–99, No.5.

21. Smith, 26, 235f. It is just possible that this model was the well-known bearded paviour George White, who often sat for Sir Joshua Reynolds, although he was a Yorkshireman (on him see W. T. Whitley, *Artists and their Friends in England*, London, 1928, II, 265–6).

22. Smith, 37.

23. A. Yarrington, I. D. Lieberman, A. Potts,
    M. Baker, 'An edition of the Ledger of Sir Francis
    Chantrey, RA at the Royal Academy, 1809–1841',
    Walpole Society, LVI, 1994, 252.
24. B. R. Haydon to Mary Mitford, 28 March 1825,
    Correspondence and Table Talk, ed. F. W. Haydon,
    London, 1876, II, 93. George Combe complained
    in 1852 that he was unable to analyse the heads of
    two lords by eye alone because of their thick hair
    (Gibbon, op. cit. II, 309).
25. For Spurzheim's lectures, B. R. Haydon, *Diary*, ed.
    W. B. Pope, Cambridge, Mass., I, 1960, 419; II,
    1960, 110 (1817). For the cast, ibid. V, 1963, 194.
    This may be either or both of the plasters of
    *c.*1820, now in the National Portrait Gallery (Fig.6)
    (D. Blayney Brown, R. Woof, S. Hebron, *Benjamin
    Robert Haydon, 1786–1846*, Grasmere, 1996, No.44).
    Haydon, *Lectures on Painting and Design*, II, London,
    1844, 62, 64. He was on friendly terms with
    G. Combe (*Diary*, 6 March 1846, V, 523f.) but
    Combe thought his knowledge of phrenology
    'only general and superficial' (Combe, 1855 cit.
    143).
26. For the Pre-Raphaelites' encounter with
    phrenology, S. Grilli, 'Pre-Raphaelitism and
    phrenology' in L. Parris (ed.), *Pre-Raphaelite Papers*,
    London, 1984, 44–60.
27. E. Williams, *Emlyn: an early Autobiography,
    1927–1935*, London, 1973, 238ff.
28. J. Epstein, *An Autobiography*, ed. R. Buckle, 2nd edn,
    London, 1963, 77–8.

Detail, Hugh Richard Fahie Hoare, (18)

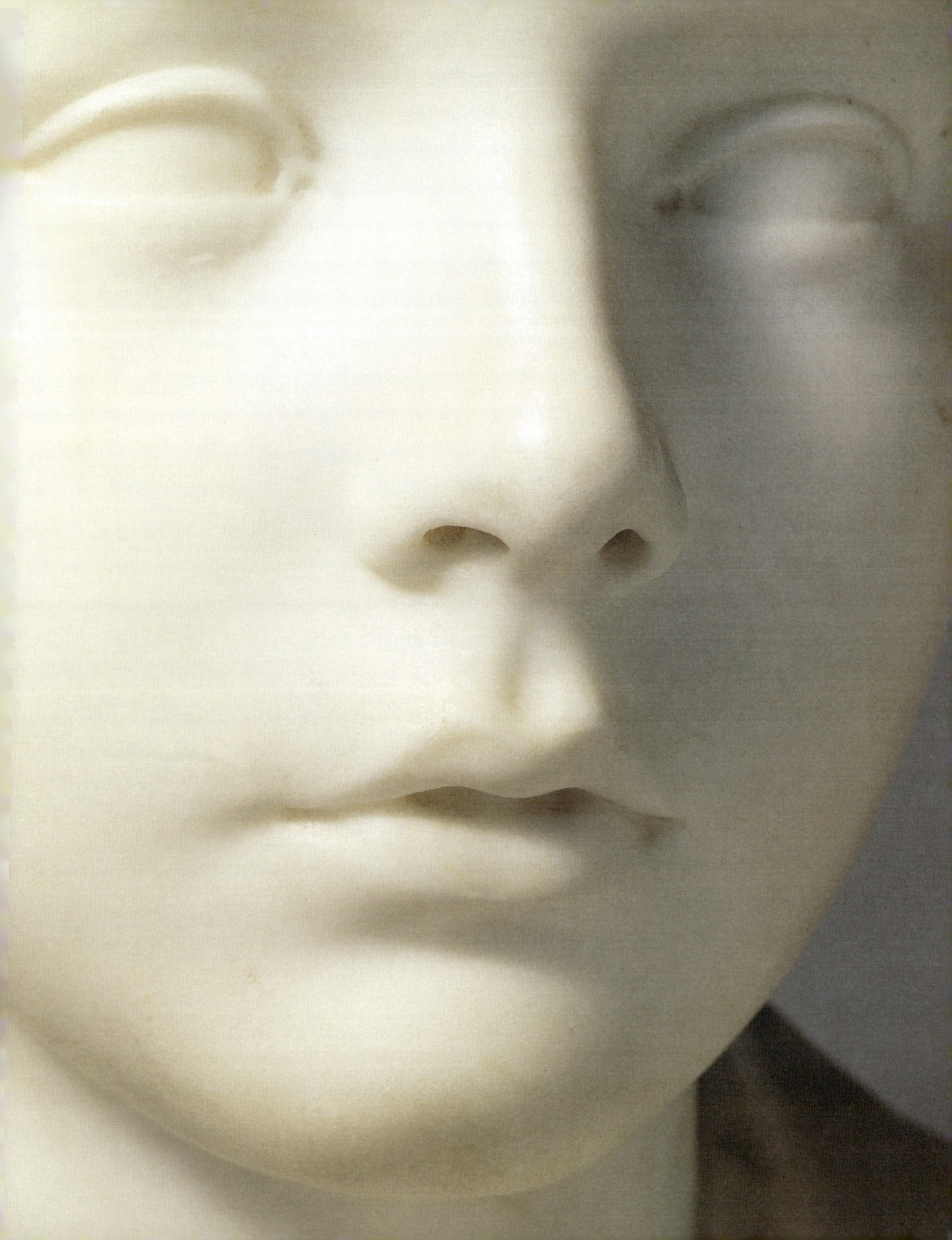

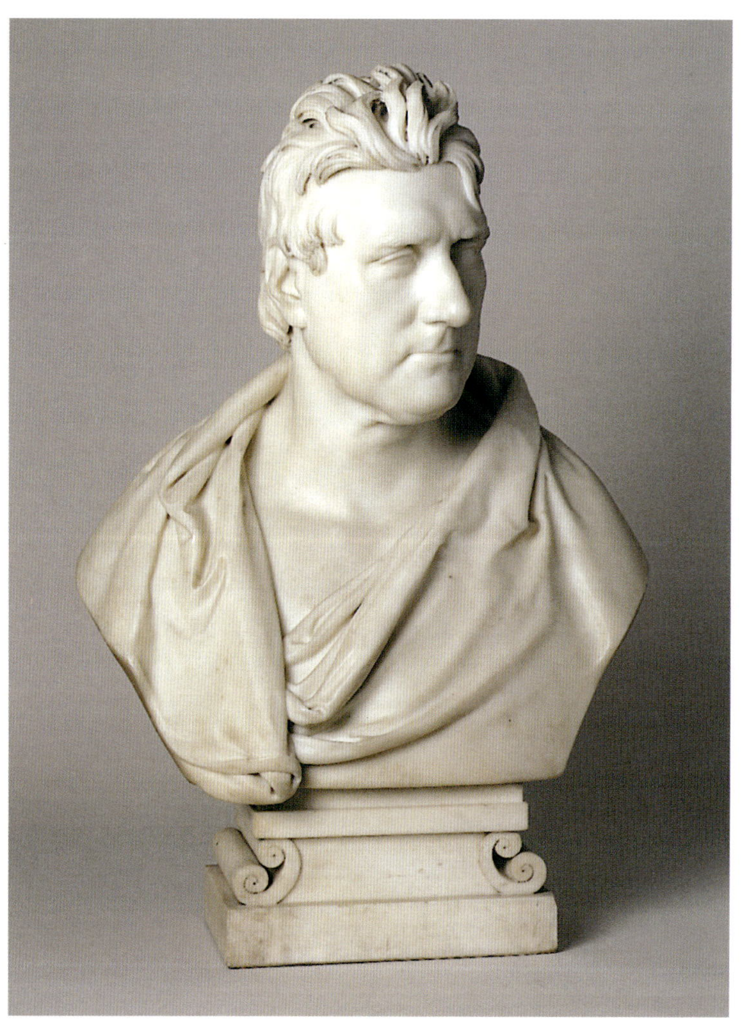

John Rennie (16)

Sir David Wilkie (13)

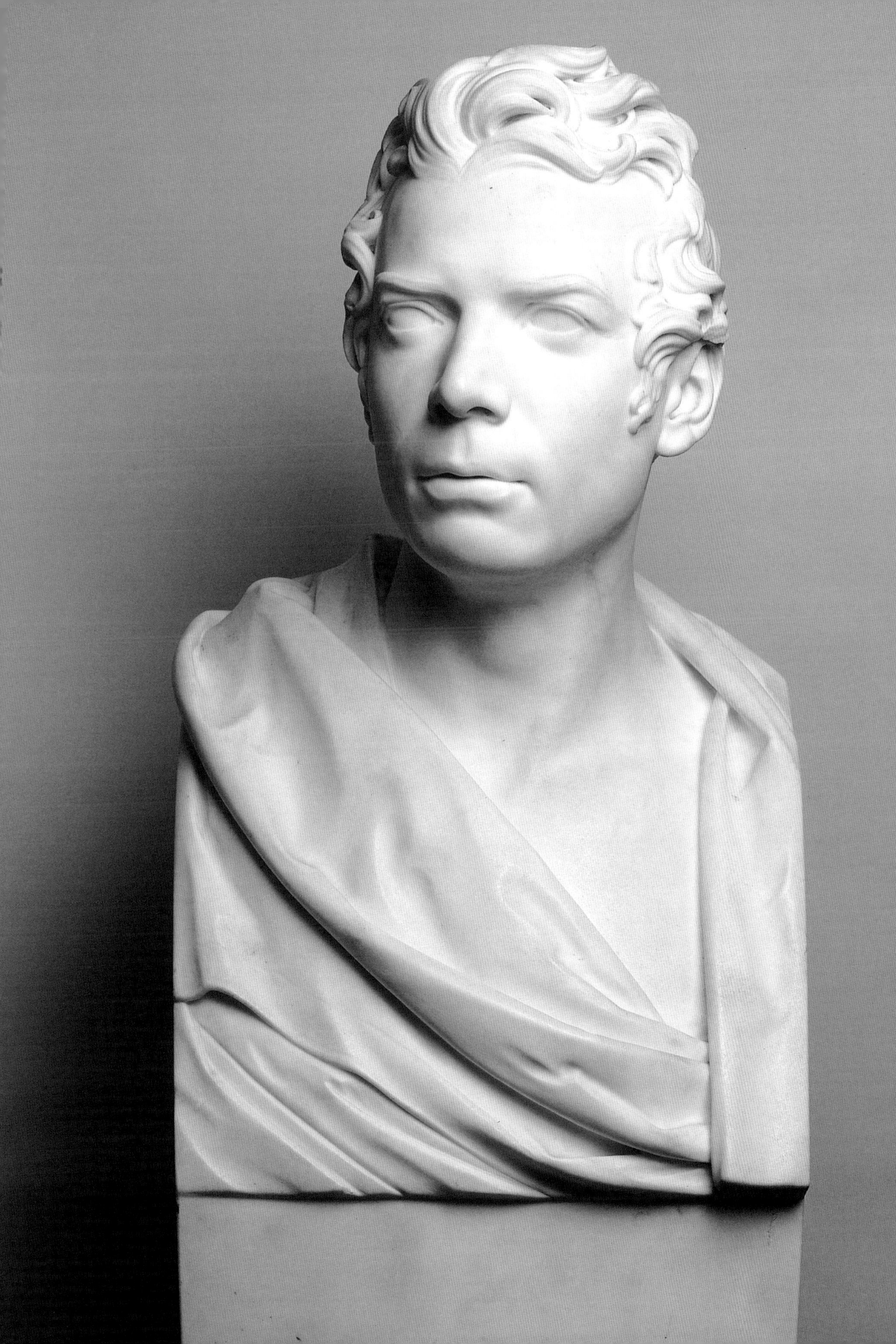

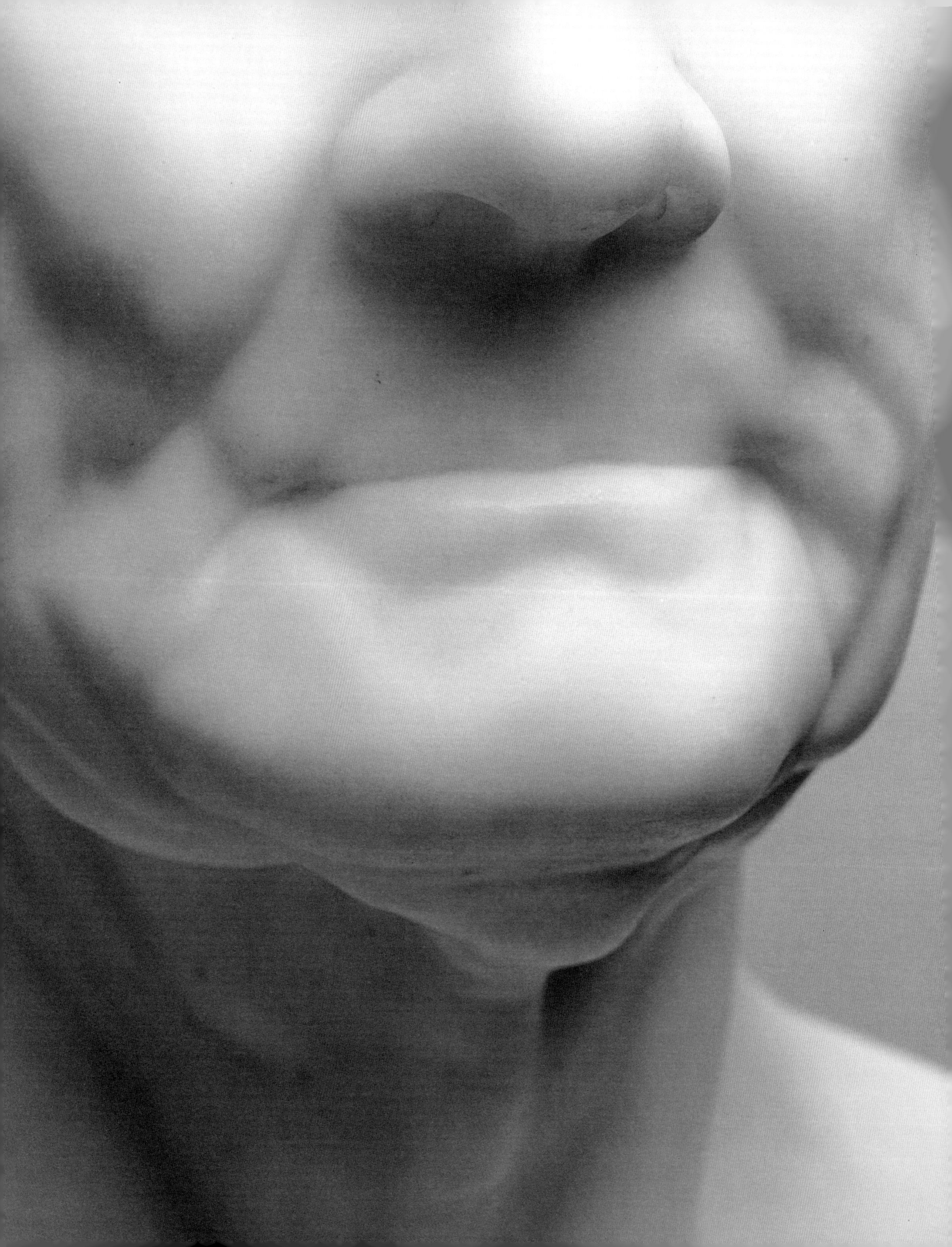

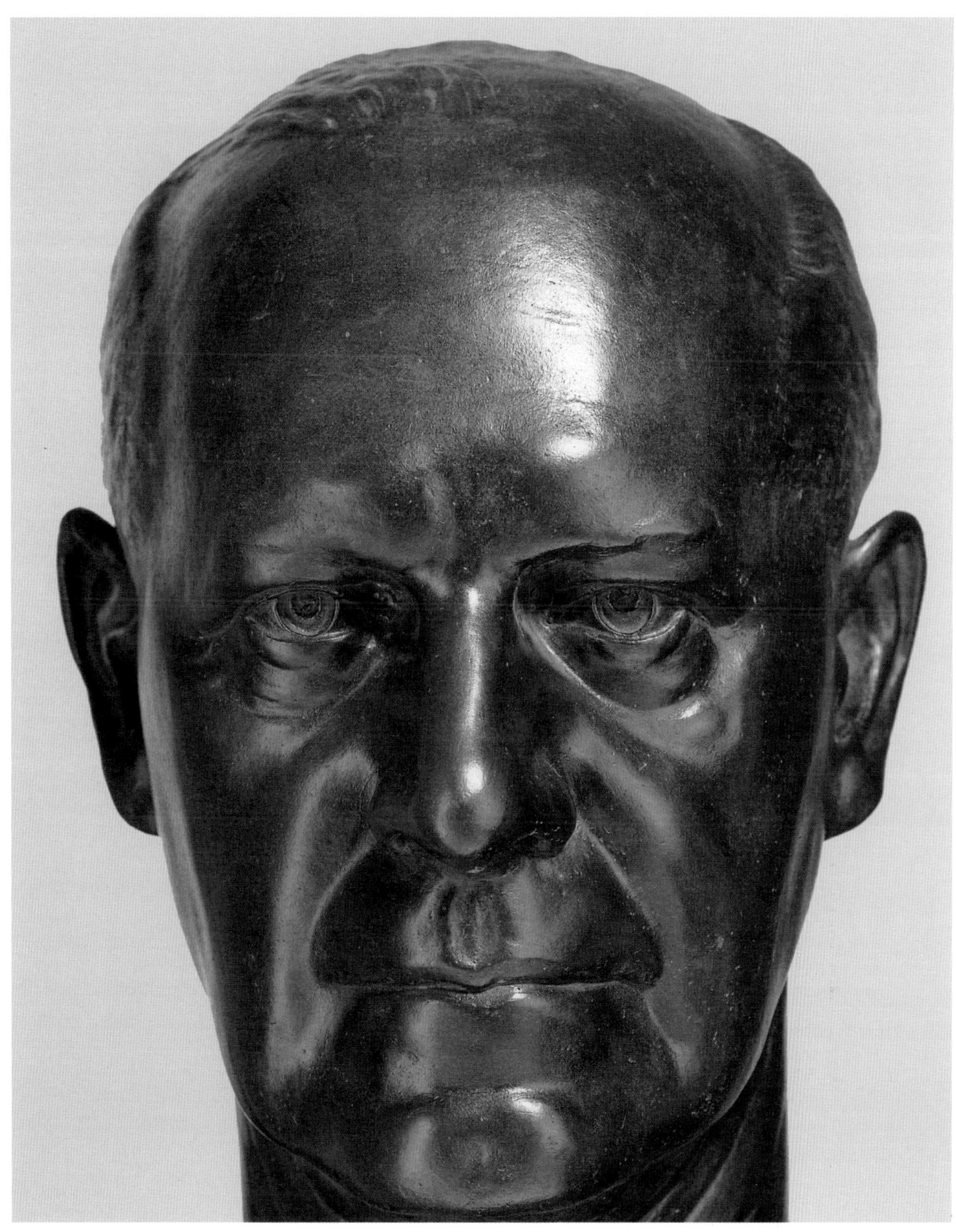

John Galsworthy, (26)

Detail, Henry Mackenzie (21)

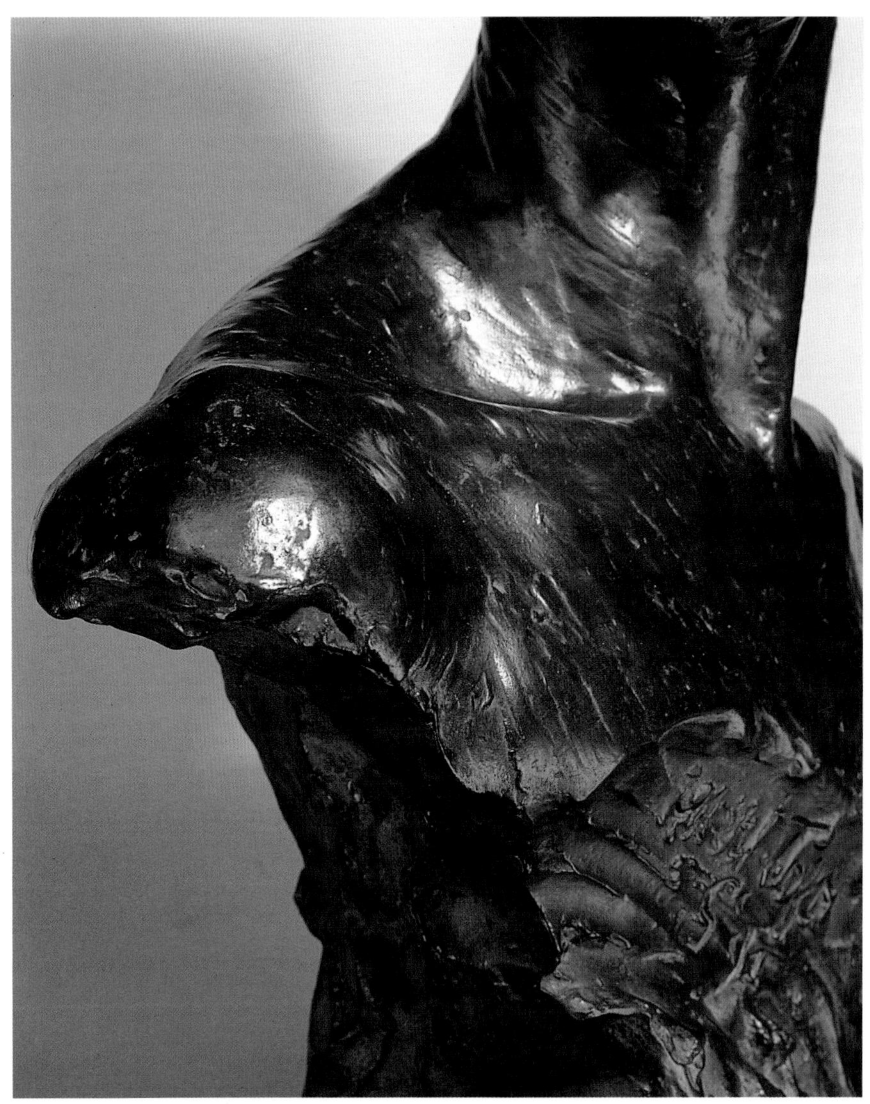

Detail, Robert Bontine Cunningham Graham (11)

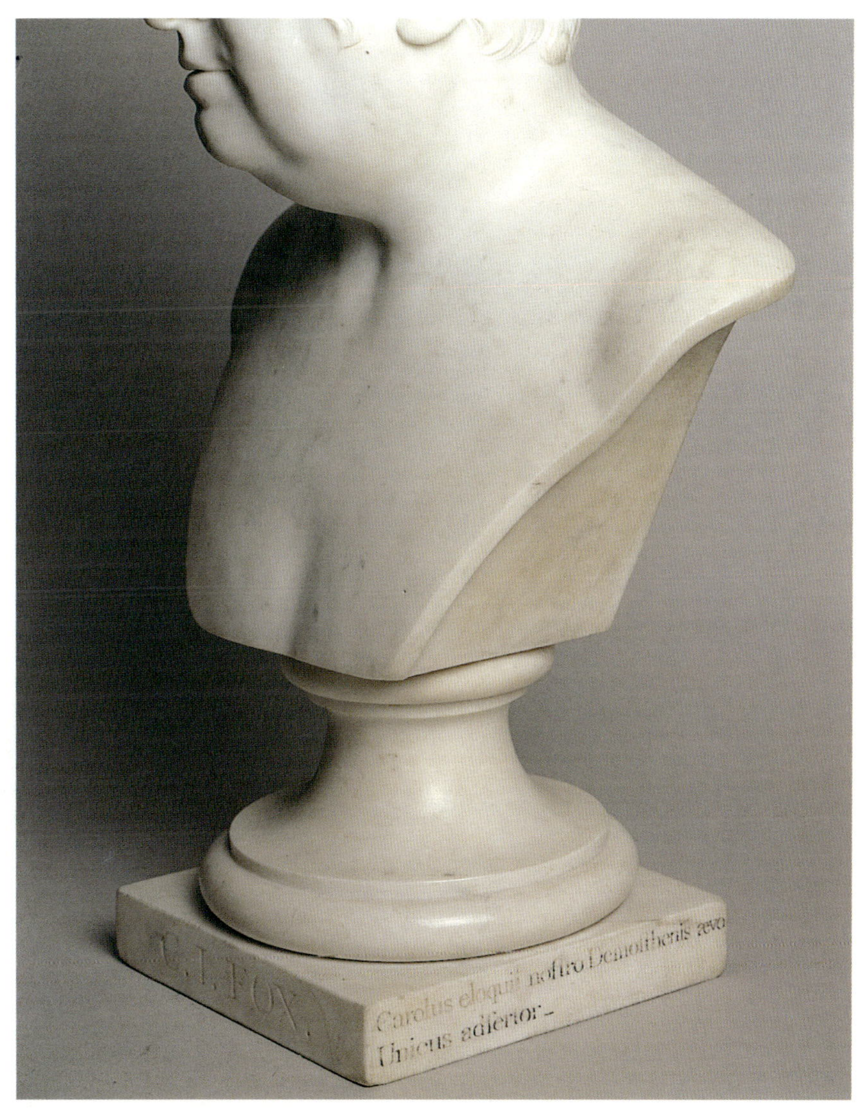

Detail, Charles James Fox (5)

Overleaf: Detail, Elizabeth Goodman Banks (23)

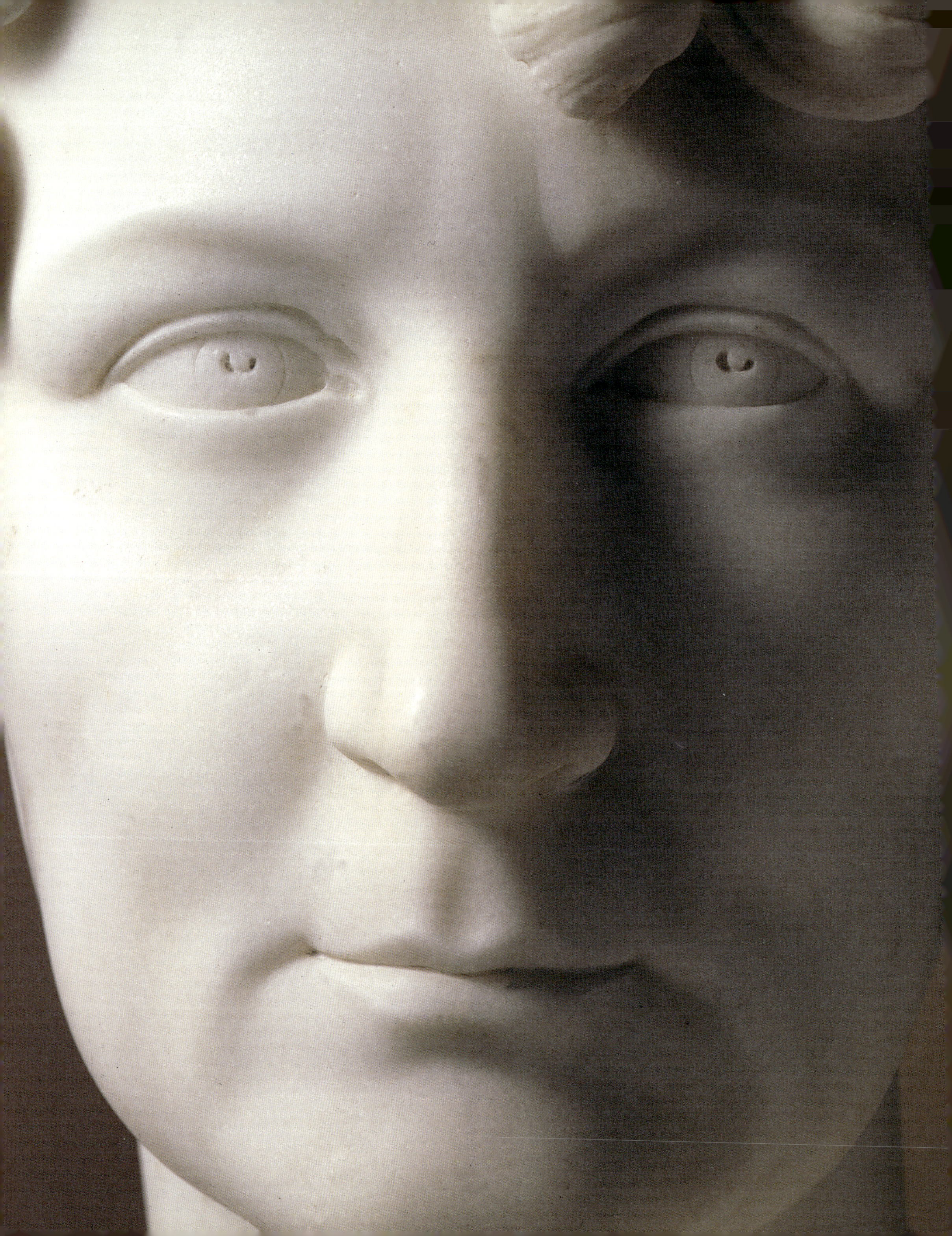

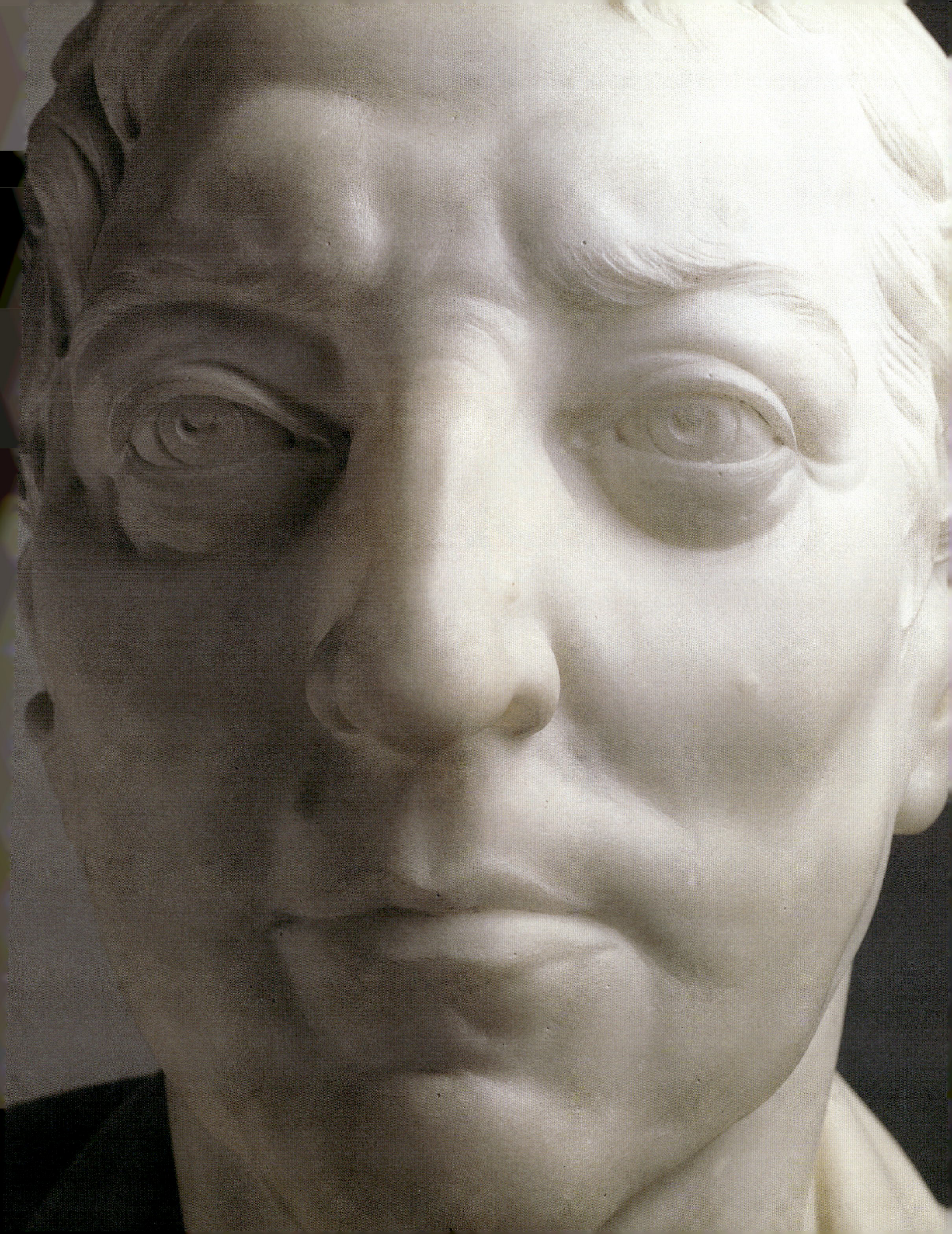

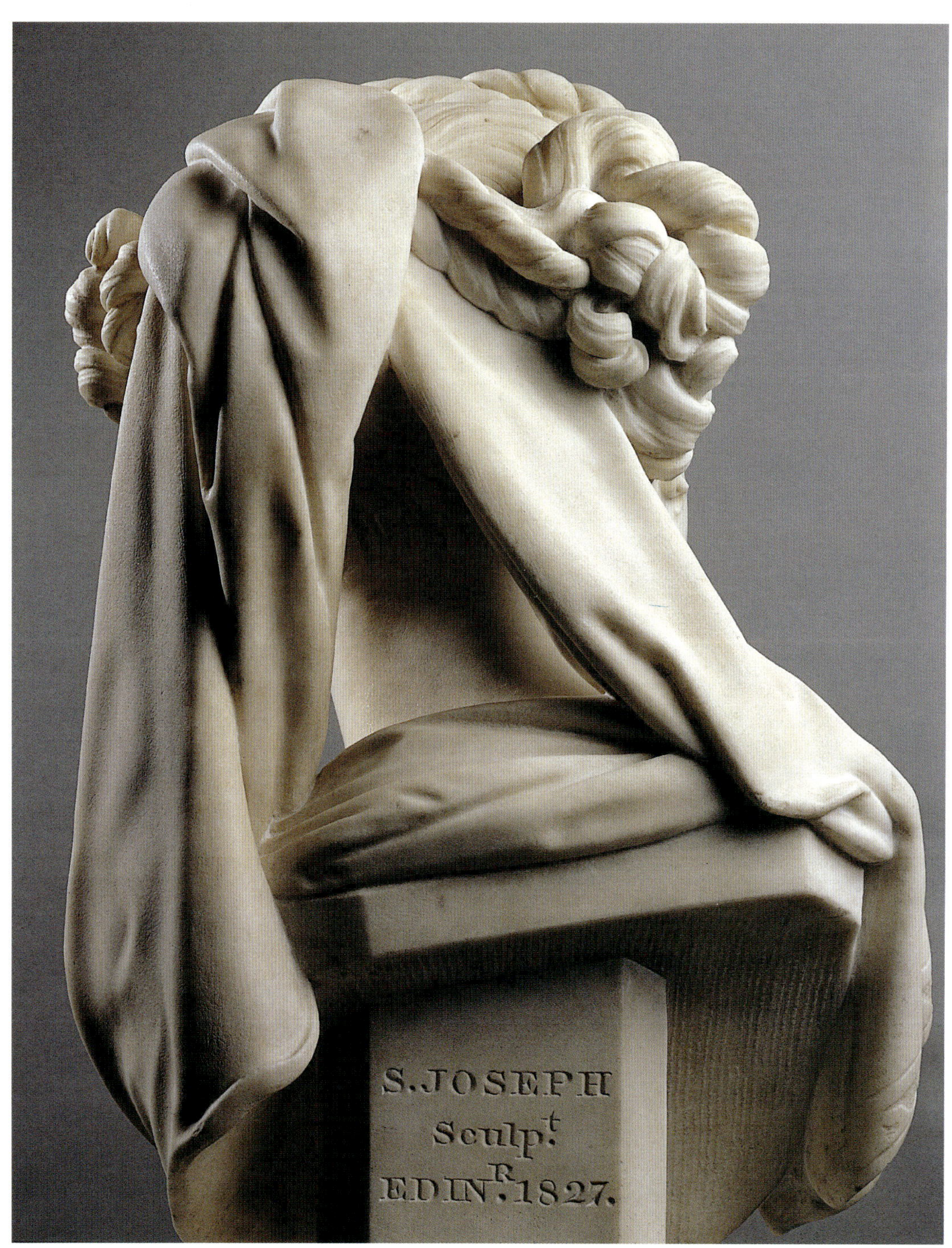

Detail, Miss Ramsay ? (10)

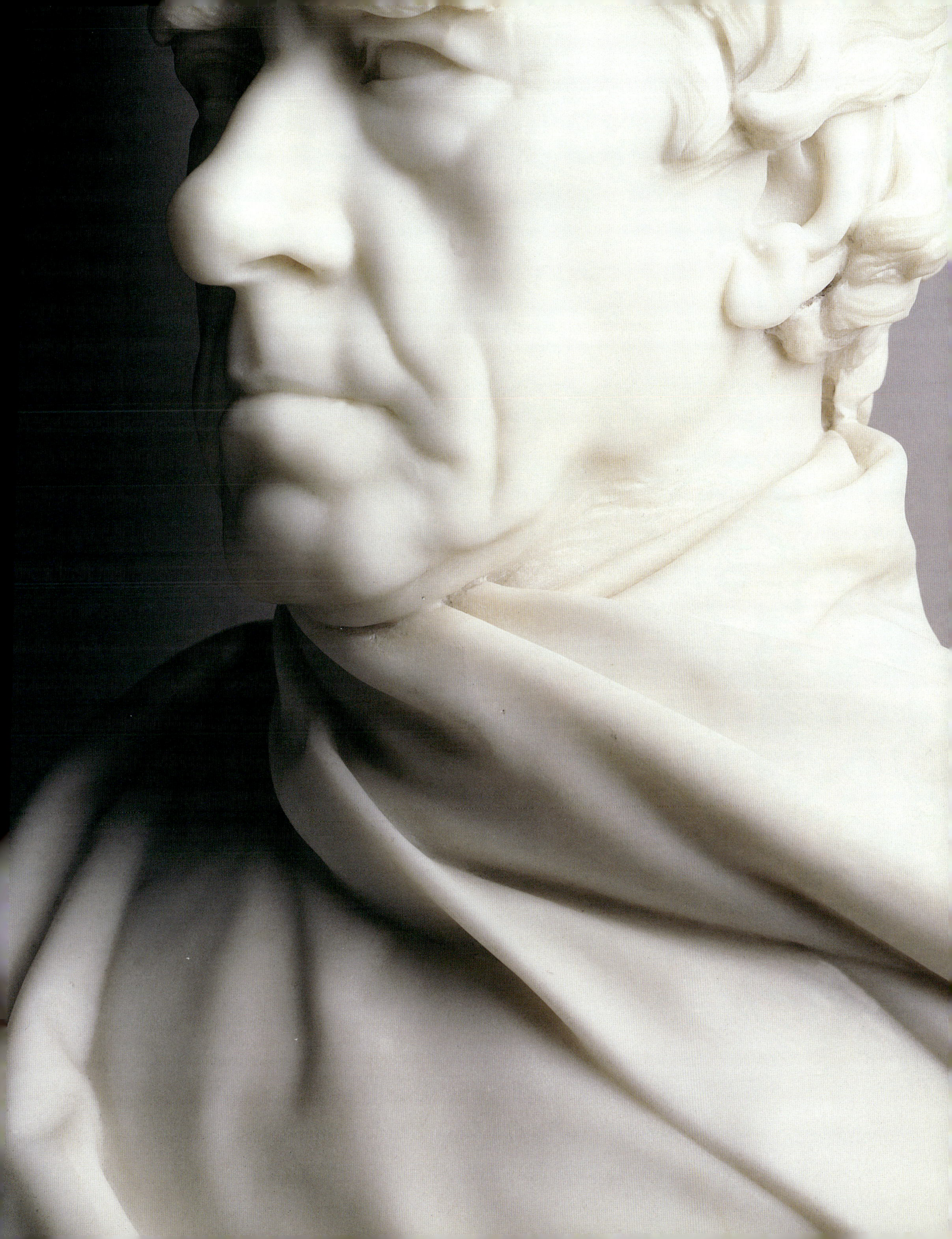

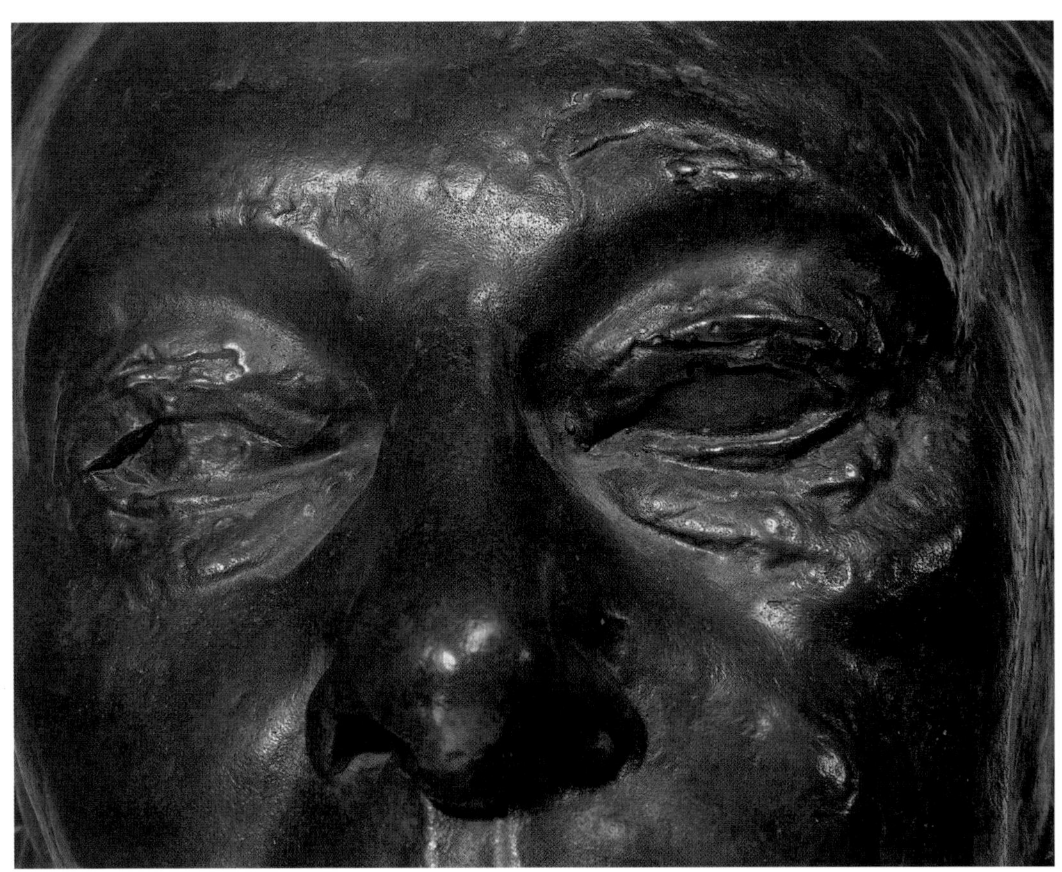

Detail, Lady Gregory (24)

LIST OF EXHIBITS

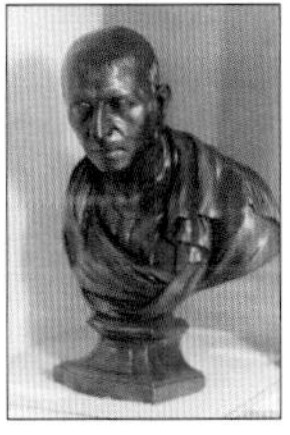

1. John Cheere (1709–87)
Cicero (106–43 BC)
*c.*1745
Painted Plaster
H 68 cm
Leeds Museums & Galleries
(Temple Newsam)

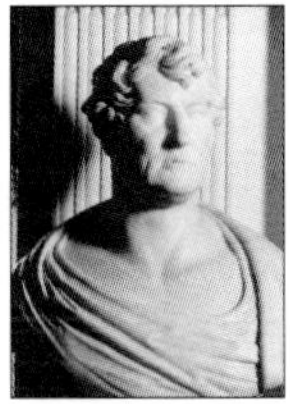

2. Joseph Gott (1786–1860)
George Banks (1777–1843)
1828
Marble
H 71 cm
Leeds Museums & Galleries
(Lotherton Hall)

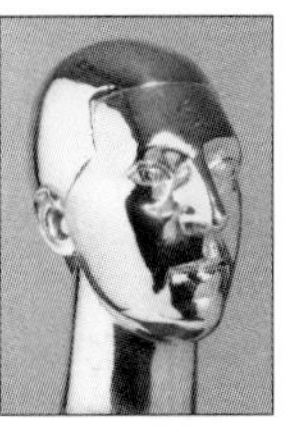

3. Frank Dobson (1886–1963)
Sir Osbert Sitwell, 5th Bt (1892–1969)
1923/1994
Modern cast of bronze bust
H 32.4 cm
National Portrait Gallery, London

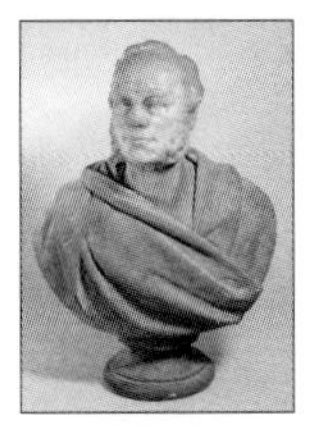

4. Edgar George Papworth (1809–66)
Unknown Man
Mid 19th century
Stone
H 74 cm
Leeds Museums & Galleries
(Leeds City Art Gallery)

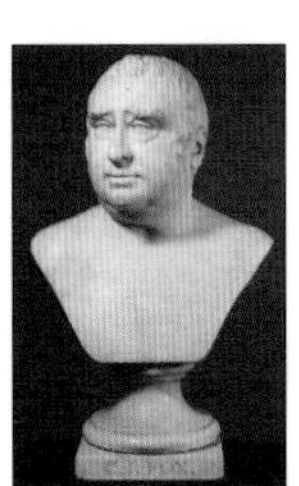

5. Joseph Nollekens (1737–1823)
Charles James Fox (1749–1806)
1805
Marble
H 67.5 cm
National Portrait Gallery, London

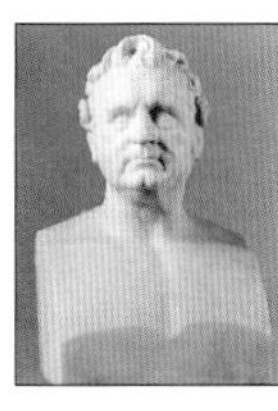

6. George MacCallum (1840–68)
David Bryce (1803–76)
1868
Marble
H 59.1 cm
National Galleries of Scotland
(Scottish National Portrait Gallery, Edinburgh)

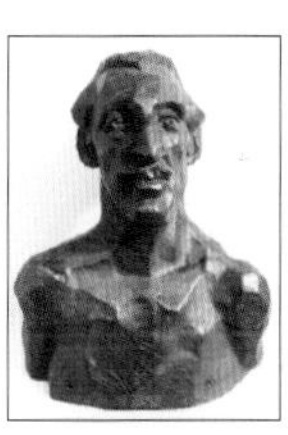

7. Henri Gaudier-Brzeska (1891–1915)
Horace Brodzky (1885–1969)
1913
Bronze
H 70 cm
Leeds Museums & Galleries
(Leeds City Art Gallery)

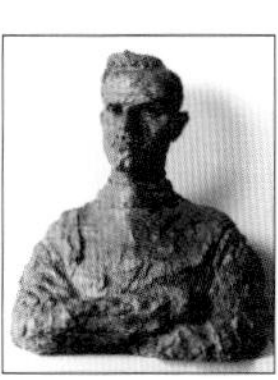

8. Sir Jacob Epstein (1880–1959)
George Black
1942
Bronze
H 64 cm
Leeds Museums & Galleries
(Leeds City Art Gallery)

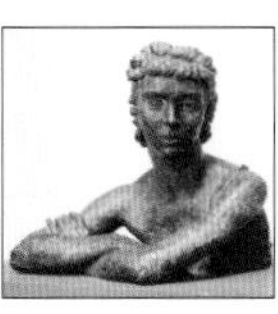

9. Frank Dobson (1886–1963)
Margaret Rawlings (b.1906)
*c.*1936
Bronze
H 58 cm
Leeds Museums & Galleries
(Leeds City Art Gallery)

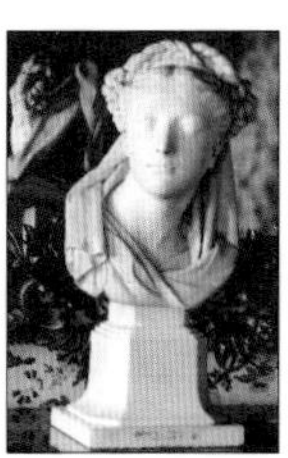

10. Samuel Joseph (1791–1850)
Miss Ramsay ?
1827
Marble
H 65 cm
Leeds Museums & Galleries
(Temple Newsam)

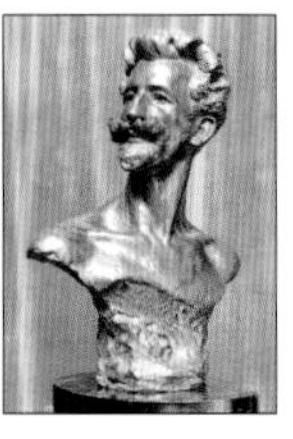

11. **Albert Toft** (1862–1949)
Robert Bontine Cunninghame Graham (1852–1936)
1891
Bronze
H 68.5 cm
National Galleries of Scotland
(Scottish National Portrait Gallery, Edinburgh)

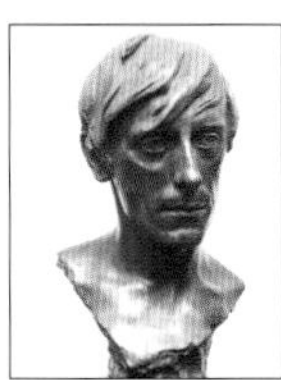

12. **Francis Derwent Wood** (1871–1926)
Ambrose McEvoy (1878–1927)
1915
Bronze
H 59.7 cm
National Portrait Gallery, London

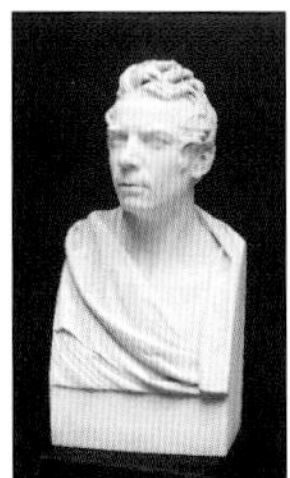

13. **Samuel Joseph** (1791–1850)
Sir David Wilkie (1785–1841)
1842
Marble
H 68.2 cm
National Galleries of Scotland
(National Gallery of Scotland, Edinburgh)

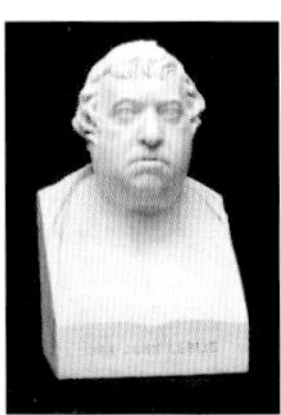

14. **John Rhind** (1828–92)
(after Samuel Joseph, 1791–1850)
Professor Sir John Leslie (1766–1832)
Date unknown
Marble
H 54 cm
National Galleries of Scotland
(Scottish National Portrait Gallery, Edinburgh)

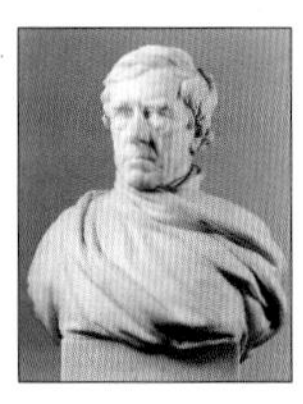

15. **John Adams Acton** (1831–1910)
*Henry Peter Brougham, 1ˢᵗ Baron, Brougham
& Vaux (1778–1868)*
1867
Marble
H 64.8 cm
National Galleries of Scotland
(Scottish National Portrait Gallery, Edinburgh)

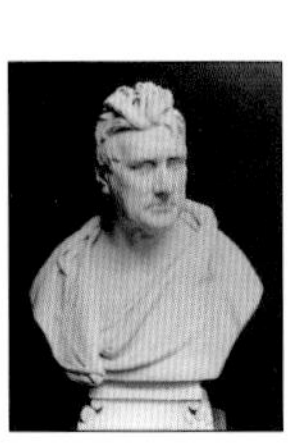

16. **Sir Francis Leggatt Chantrey** (1781–1841)
John Rennie (1785–1821)
1818
Marble
H 63 cm
National Portrait Gallery, London

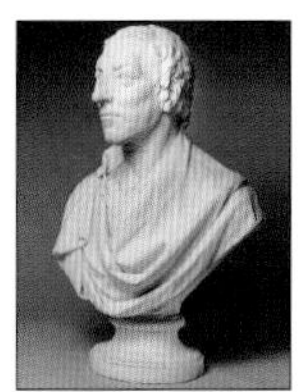

17. **Joseph Wilton** (1722–1803)
William Pitt, 1ˢᵗ Earl of Chatham (1708–78)
c.1759
Marble
H 76.2 cm
National Portrait Gallery, London

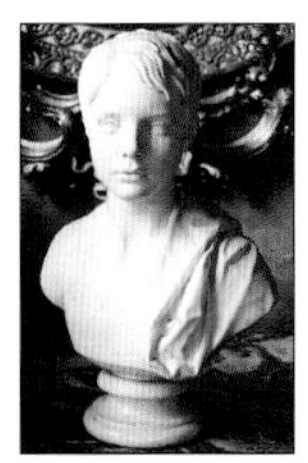

18. **Henry Weekes** (1807–77)
Hugh Richard Fahie Hoare (1827–40)
1840
Marble
H 63 cm
Leeds Museums & Galleries
(Lotherton Hall)

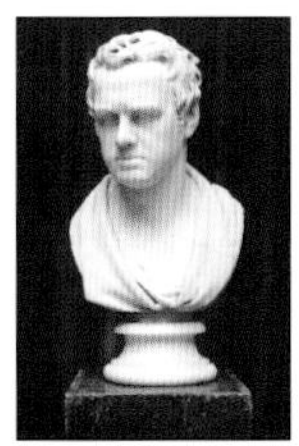

19. **Sir Francis Leggatt Chantrey** (1781–1841)
Francis Horner (1778–1817)
1818
Marble
H 61 cm
National Galleries of Scotland
(Scottish National Portrait Gallery, Edinburgh)

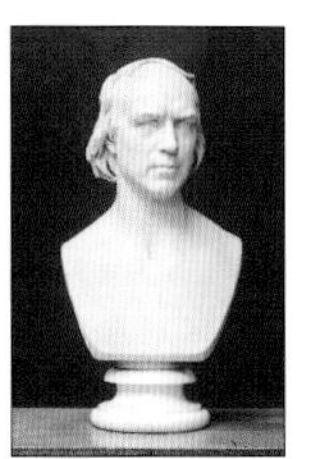

20. **Henry Weekes** (1807–77)
Allan Cunningham (1784–1842)
1842
Marble
H 73 cm
National Galleries of Scotland
(Scottish National Portrait Gallery, Edinburgh)

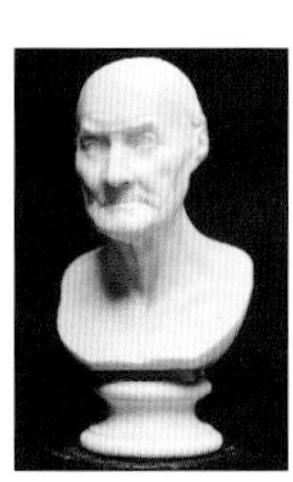

21. **Samuel Joseph** (1791–1850)
Henry Mackenzie (1745–1831)
Date not known
Marble
H 55.2 cm
National Galleries of Scotland
(Scottish National Portrait Gallery, Edinburgh)

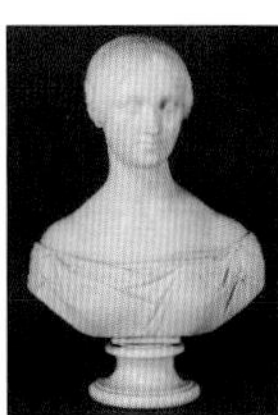

22. **Richard James Wyatt** (1795–1850)
Bust of a Woman
Date not known
Marble
H 61.5 cm
Leeds Museums & Galleries
(Temple Newsam)

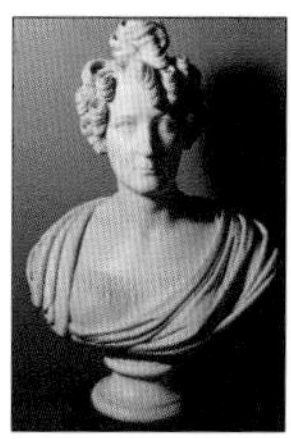

23. **Joseph Gott** (1786–1860)
Elizabeth Goodman Banks (1781–1853)
1828
Marble
H 71 cm
Leeds Museums & Galleries
(Lotherton Hall)

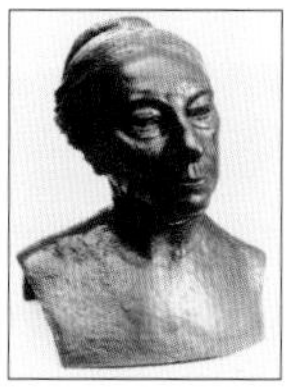

24. **Sir Jacob Epstein** (1880–1959)
Lady Gregory (1859–1932)
1911
Bronze
H 40 cm
Leeds Museums & Galleries
(Leeds City Art Gallery)

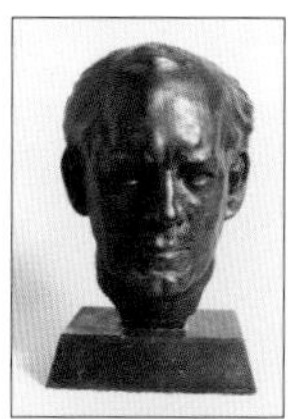

25. **Kathleen Scott** (1878–1947)
John Galsworthy (1867–1933)
c.1920
Bronze
H 34 cm
Leeds Museums & Galleries
(Leeds City Art Gallery)

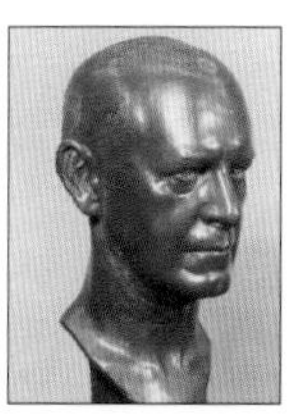

26. **David Evans** (1894–1959)
John Galsworthy (1867–1933)
1929
Bronze
H 54 cm
National Portrait Gallery, London

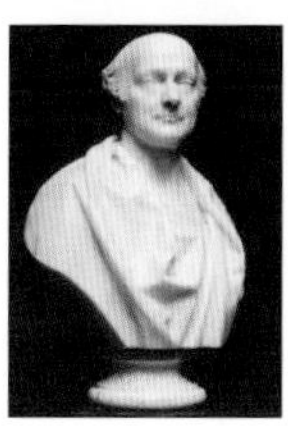

27. **Patric Park** (1811–55)
James Jardine (1776–1858)
1842
Marble
H 73.6 cm
National Galleries of Scotland
(Scottish National Portrait Gallery, Edinburgh)

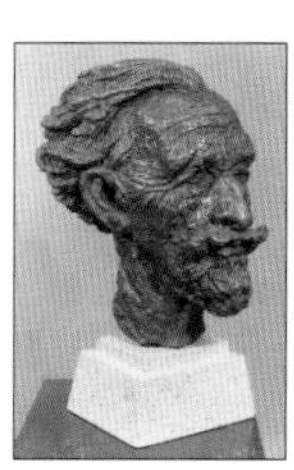

28. **Sir Jacob Epstein** (1880–1959)
*Robert Bontine Cunninghame Graham
(1852–1936)*
1923
Bronze
H 35 cm
National Portrait Gallery, London

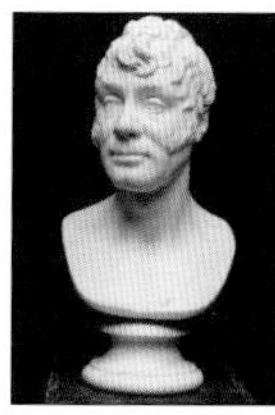

29. **Joseph Nollekens** (1737–1823)
*James Maitland, 8th Earl of Lauderdale
(1759–1839)*
1803
Marble
H 54.5 cm
National Galleries of Scotland
(Scottish National Portrait Gallery, Edinburgh)

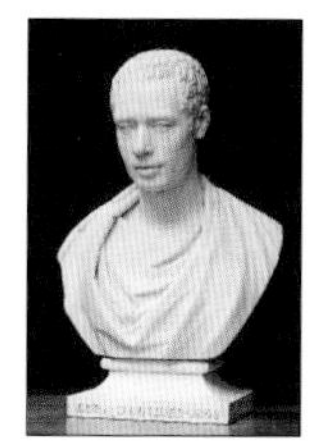

30. **Lawrence Macdonald** (1799–1878)
George Combe (1788–1858)
Date not known
Marble
H 69.4 cm
National Galleries of Scotland
(Scottish National Portrait Gallery, Edinburgh)

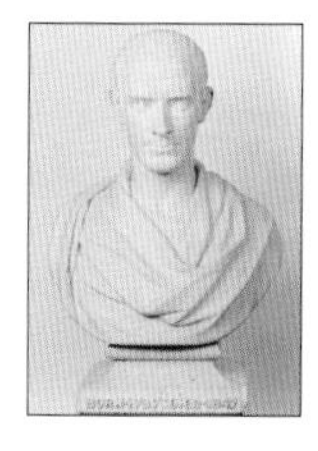

31. **John Hutchison** (1840–1908)
Andrew Combe (1797–1847)
1889
Marble
H 70.02 cm
National Galleries of Scotland
(Scottish National Portrait Gallery, Edinburgh)

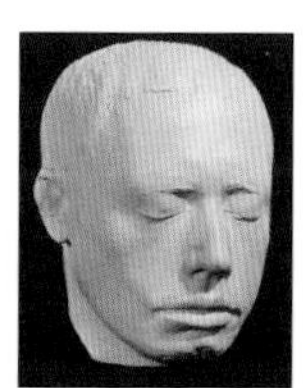

32. **Life Mask of George Combe** (replica)
1824
Plaster
H 25 cm
William Ramsay Henderson Trust

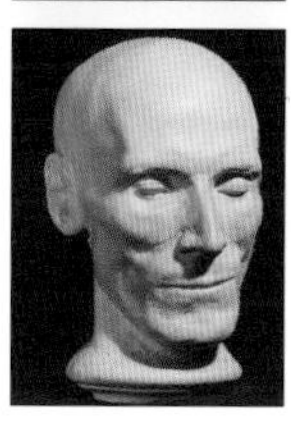

33. **Death Mask of Dr Andrew Combe**
(replica)
1847
Plaster
H 29 cm
William Ramsay Henderson Trust

Published to accompany the exhibition **Return to Life: A New Look at the Portrait Bust**
produced by the Henry Moore Institute, Leeds, the National Portrait Gallery, London and
the Scottish National Portrait Gallery, Edinburgh

Exhibition Venues:

Henry Moore Institute	**27 September 2000 – 7 January 2001**
National Portrait Gallery	**7 February – 20 May 2001**
Scottish National Portrait Gallery	**21 June – 23 September 2001**

Curated by Penelope Curtis, Henry Moore Institute, Peter Funnell, National Portrait Gallery
and Nicola Kalinsky, Scottish National Portrait Gallery with assistance from Gill Armstrong
and Stephen Feeke (HMI), Kathleen Soriano (NPG) and Susanna Kerr (SNPG)

London showing sponsored by Phillip Mould, Historical Portraits

Catalogue prepared and published in Great Britain by
the Henry Moore Institute, 74 The Headrow, Leeds, LS1 3AH

ISBN 1 900081 67 9

Edited by the curators with assistance from
Gill Armstrong and Stephen Feeke
Picture research by Liz Aston

Designed by Raymond Carpenter
Typeset by Tom Knott
Printed by Richard Edward Ltd

Collection photography: © the respective institution,
including specially commissioned photography (pp. 49–60) by Jerry Hardman-Jones

Cover images:
John Adams Acton, *Henry Peter Brougham, 1ˢᵗ Baron Brougham & Vaux*, 1867,
National Galleries of Scotland (Scottish National Portrait Gallery)
David Evans, *John Galsworthy*, 1929, National Portrait Gallery

Photographs illustrating the texts were supplied by the owners,
with the exception of the following:

'*A Sort of Corporate Company*' by Malcolm Baker:
FIG.1 From *The London County Council Survey of London*, Vol. III;
'The Parish of St. Giles-in-the-Fields', Part 1, 'Lincoln's Inn Fields, London', 1912
FIG.10 Julian Nieman/Country Life Picture Library
FIG.11 Stanley Eost/Paul Mellon Centre, London
FIG.12 Jerry Hardman-Jones

Busts and Identity by John Gage:
FIG.2 From *Essays on Physiognomy*, London, 1789, ref, L.R.225.d.10.
FIG.3 From *Elements of Phrenology*, Edinburgh & London, 1824, ref. 784.e.3.
FIG.5 © English Heritage
FIG.8 © Estate of Jacob Epstein/Tate Gallery, London, 2000